A PLACE TO CALL *Home:*

The Story Of How A Tv Series
Stirred Passions And Connections

DONNA ROBINSON DIVINE
AND RONNI KRASNOW, EDITORS

FORWARD

Where did she come from, that woman leaving European horrors to sail towards Australian hope? Where did they come from, that family changed irrevocably by encountering her aboard ship? Sarah Adams and the Bligh family. And by expansion, Inverness, the country town where they melded and morphed. Where did the world of what was originally titled "Another Country" come from? The world of "A Place to Call Home".

I believe every writer saves a fortune in therapy costs, by processing their confusion and disfunction onto the page, by visiting the grab bag of their inherited neuroses, selecting as seems valuable and examining, as these flaws, foibles and fears are reshaped into characters and narrative. This process is sometimes conscious, more often not. I certainly know for myself that every show I have created has been a part of my on-going process of understanding who the closeted gay boy, who felt alienated from his loving family and social network in lower middle-class Perth, was and is. How did he travel from a limited life in a relatively poor family in a post war suburb in the most geographically isolated capital city in the world, to a successful creator of numerous television shows that frequently defined the entertainment zeitgeist of his country?

Sarah and the Bligh family and Inverness and its residents, and the narrative woven around them, are the answer to those questions distilled into the most significant creation of my career.

Without going into too much detail, to risk the embarrassment of overshare, Sarah was the damaged closeted me, who survived youthful shame to find love and warmth in a seemingly forbidden relationship. Elizabeth was the judgmental and censorious world that said to me that my history excluded me from being worthy of a deep and abiding love. George was the decent and loving man, who could see past my damage to the real me, the me worth loving, the man who would defy the, until recently, gay hating society by loving me. James Bligh was my internalised homophobia, that self-hate a hateful society had instilled in me, the feelings I had to overcome to see myself as equal to or possibly better than heterosexual men. James and Olivia's journey from lovers to deep loving friends, stronger for the confusions they shared, was a complete parallel to the relationship I have shared with the great love of my life, once my partner, now my bulwark in the crazy sea of life.

Combine this therapy through narrative with a wish to pay homage to my parents' generation and the strength they showed in the adversity of war and post war life, and the characters, themes and settings of "A Place to Call Home" emerged from the fog of creative options. The names of my dear departed relatives show how I sampled the past to create a fiction. My Uncles Roy and Jack, my Aunts Elizabeth and Doris, the surnames Adams and Collins, all from the family tree. The essence of my wonderful father Bert, one of the truly good men who have lived, channeled into Roy Briggs, the essence of my mother Poppy, channeled into Sarah, the strong woman she would have been if life and circumstance had not limited her options and drowned her in unspoken regrets.

Therein lay the fuel of the nuclear reactor of "A Place to Call Home", always informing the sprawling saga with the radiation it generated, dampened to greater and lesser extent by the carbon rods of thoughts from other minds contributing to the process. I must give credit to a number of those minds. Katherine Thomson, the wonderful co-writer of Seasons Four through Six. Chris Martin Jones, the invaluable producer throughout. Julie McGauran, my support always at Channel 7. Brian Walsh, who rescued the story from the oblivion of cancellation by commissioning its continuation on Foxtel. Penny Winn, head of drama at Foxtel, who contributed through her perception and trust. Susan Bower, who stepped into the very difficult role of taking up the narrative torch for Season 3.

And finally, to the whole deliriously wonderful cast, for their contributions beyond compare. Where would any of us be without them? So much personal investment from my soul, so much total commitment from theirs to bring the page to life. No wonder the show transcended its basic elements to become truly universal drama.

And from this flowed the love and commitment that came from our viewers. To know that my journey from a confused closeted gay boy in Perth led me to write something that has touched hearts worldwide makes me know the true worth of creativity. This will be among the few truly essential final thoughts I will gather to allow satisfaction whenever my final moments come.

Thank you, dear fans, for embracing the show and allowing this to be so.

Bevan Lee

INTRODUCTION:

Wars end, but not with winners and losers so much as people, scattered, scarred, and numbed. Shout-outs of mission accomplished invoke not yearnings for peace but rather threats of annihilation. Religious doctrines, dismissed as irrelevant at best, are called out as brutal and dehumanizing at worst. To win elections, politicians issue messages poisonous to a shared culture. An era expected to open up a glorious sense of destiny is replaced by an age dominated by a dread running as deep as the forecasts of an unnerving descent into anarchy. This is as much a description of 1953 Australia in the television series, A Place To Call Home, as it is of today's world. It is not the first time the universe, itself, has become a zone of turbulence, its inhabitants, beset by uncertainty, ironically finding the script for their inner turmoil cast in fiction.

A Place To Call Home begins on a ship when a nurse—Sister Adams by name--works her passage home to Australia to console her mother who is grieving for a son killed in the Korean War. Estranged from her family, she stands before the welcome mat, fearful of what she will find inside and wondering whether her mother will accept her after a breach of decades. Several minutes into their reunion, the mother tells her daughter to leave because she cannot abide a child, born a Catholic, who is now—a Jew.

No one better embodies the opening of Australian society than Sister Sarah Adams, at the

beginning of the series as much an outsider by class as by the act that made her a Jew. Love brought Sarah to Judaism, and Judaism enabled Sarah to grow up, learn languages, engage in battle, and form an identity that lived more dangerously and looked more deeply into abysses than most people could imagine. Born and raised in Sydney but feeling uncomfortable with the rigid Catholic pietism of her mother, Sarah travels to Europe, becomes a nurse, embarks on a romantic quest to fight fascism in Spain and in France before being captured by the Nazis and sent to Ravensbruck Concentration Camp. She crosses religious lines for love, but with or without her Jewish husband, she retains a fierce loyalty to her adopted religion even though it caused such a painful rupture with her mother.

On the ship, Sister Adams is asked to care for Elizabeth Bligh, the matriarch of a wealthy landed family returning to Australia with son and granddaughter as well as with newly wedded grandson and his wife, a marriage intended to blunt his desire for sexual relations with men. Acutely conscious of the privileges bestowed on the Bligh family, matriarch Elizabeth also embraces a set of traditions coiled around a social structure that is expected to ensure stability from the particularly harrowing experiences of a world war exposing country and people to assaults on all fronts including the ones at home.

The encounter between Sarah and Elizabeth reflects the strains and conflicts that hovered over Australia in the years following the traumas of war, their undiminished echo shaping lives and hardening the fault lines. Everyone watching this program knows how the narrative ends for Australia, but few understand what it took to make room in the country for people typically hidden from view or told, in one way or another, that they didn't count for much. The freedoms taken for granted today were won in painful struggles too often measured only as gains without taking a full accounting of losses.

The Blighs live much of their lives within a mansion—called Ash Park—possessed of wealth and status from acres of land where their sheep graze until shorn of their wool and sold off at an auction proclaiming the family's economic might. Their apocryphal town of Inverness contains no ground plan of the cluster of roads and churches or of its railway station carrying residents to Sydney for business, pleasure, and freedom. When the poor walk into Ash Park, they enter mostly as servants, stable hands, or chauffeurs; when they pray in churches, they sit crowded in pews behind the notable families always conscious of the social code and etiquette that draw distinct hierarchical lines even before their God.

In 1953, Australians lived in the shadow of experiences they could not fully explain: the war to which so many young men and women had gone ended up producing more desolation and grief than peace and comfort. Church and family could not offer adequate explanations for the past nor did they continue to serve as the absolute constituents of destiny given the social and political pressures pushing upward and outward against the constraints of class and circumstance. An open society not only posed dangers to traditional class and culture; it also raised fears about what the forces blowing in the wind would bring or where they would take people and society. Would the emancipatory dreams of the poor and exploited be realized and would they march everyone to the edge of a chaotic precipice? Was a bell tolling for all that Australians believed would last forever?

Even as it was on the cusp of extinction, the way of life, portrayed in this series, was ended without the world crashing down, and the story told over the six seasons on television peels back the present to reveal a past that explains why change may be more frightening to think about than to live through. The very first episode opens with these words: 'The past is a foreign country. They do things differently,' seemingly drawing a sharp distinction between past and present. But the quotation is from L. P. Hartley's 1953 book, The Go-Between, and the title is a metaphor for many different kinds of bridges linking people and circumstance. As A Place To Call Home unfolds, it becomes clear that radical change requires not only a reckoning with the past but also an acknowledgement of its heavy weight on the present.

What A Place To Call Home does so brilliantly is to capture history, in all its messiness, and turn it into a narrative that has power. How an Australian society once taking for granted that Jews and homosexuals threatened its social order and collective morality was persuaded to embrace the diversity it feared is the question at the center of the narrative. How did outsiders marginalized because of class, religion, or sexual identity by a social structure designating landed families as custodians of stability, identity, and values emerge to be seen and heard? Because the war that so radically redistributed power brought the country's fissures into sharp relief, elites could not claw back the power they once exercised over family, class, gender, and sex. Nor in this postwar period could new expressions of love be ignored, denied, or banished, changes terrifying the people clinging to the blessings provided by a stable moral center, whatever its flaws.

The question of what it takes to hold together a society, then, is everywhere in A Place To Call Home. The program can no more get away from this topic than it can from the memory of the past and its soul-crushing discrimination. But the past is also entangled with a memory of a time when social ties still counted for something, and when families bestowed on their members a web of emotion and duty. The past leaves as much a legacy of possibility as of assault and humiliation.

The possibilities drawn from the past are there in A Place To Call Home. They are emphatically there with Sarah. Born as Bridget, Sarah takes a new name when she is born again as a Jew but then, curiously, returns to her birthplace in search of a home. Sarah must learn that a home is not so much found as created. Marking Shabbat helps forge a community evoking for Sarah both the happy celebrations before the war and the dark times in the camps when Jewish women were killed and humiliated simply for remembering their Sabbath by following the time-honored ritual of lighting candles. Shabbat enables Sarah to talk a bit about surviving the war and the damage done to her in Ravensbruck. Sarah must call up the horrors of the war before she can live both with her own feelings about what she had to do to survive and with the wounds she still carries. Through this process, she begins to realize that the past cannot be totally buried because the trauma wrapped around it can, without giving notice, break through to the surface.

Sarah Adams is defined, initially, as a threat to the old order, but she becomes a model for the new one, a transformation symbolized by her recitation of the Kaddish. In Judaism, Kaddish often serves as a kind of comma, allowing worshippers to pause after completing one set of prayers before beginning another. Although conventionally understood as a prayer in memory of the dead, Kaddish contains no reference to death. When someone dies, Jews are called on to say Kaddish to affirm before their community a commitment to live a life of moral purpose even while the text acknowledges God's distance as much as God's presence. In embracing this practice, Sarah shows how even the most profound rupture can become a source of spiritual renewal. As the prayer threads through the several seasons, it also shows what is necessary for a place to become, fully and meaningfully, a home. In season one, Sarah recites Kaddish, alone, marking the death of her mother. By the third season, the residents of Inverness—some who initially found Jewish customs strange—call on a Rabbi to bring a quorum [minyan] of Jewish males to Inverness to help Sarah observe Jewish mourning practices after her husband's death. Kaddish is a prayer that requires a communal response. There is as much need for Sarah to develop a voice that can be heard in her community--wherever it is or however it is composed--as there is for the community to respond and say Amen.

To return this introduction to where it began is to acknowledge the importance of family restructured and reconceived in a land not quarantined against the ideas racing across other continents, and where people listen and respect each other's stories without changing them. Telling stories of people once seemingly driven out of existence acknowledges not only that they meant something to one another but also that they mattered for a later time and a later generation.

Human beings are storytellers. Narratives construct the world in which we live. Traumas for people like Sarah, originally from a working-class family who became a Jew by choice shatter conventional narratives. The only way she can live and find fulfillment is both to face and share her experiences and ultimately to insert them into the story of a place that can then be made into a home.

Finally, any accounting of this Program must ask why such a quintessentially Australian story about mid-twentieth century traumas has so much to say to people in the twenty-first and why it so deeply struck a chord with people living far removed from the land framing this series. A Place To Call Home speaks across time and space because it offers a mirror to people who see in it their own reflection. It enables them to draw their own map of dislocation and pain but also to chart their own way out. In Israel, one of the 140 countries streaming the program, A Place To Call Home's title is translated as Makom ba-lev [literally, a place in the heart] meaning that a place to call home is connected to body and soul, imprinted on the heart as well as on the mind turning the idea of place into the foundation for a coherent story and no less important, for the kind of home that gives what people desperately want and need—a sense of belonging.

THE CANCELLATION:

I n the midst of the second season of A Place To Call Home, Channel 7 announced the program would not be included in its lineup for the next year. The decision to cancel the series upset cast and crew and enraged fans. The magnitude of the program's narrative was matched by the intensity of the passion of the people who understood that this story about Australia's past had vital meaning for its present. I have no access to negotiations to preserve the show transpiring behind the scenes. There is, however, a public record of why the program generated such strong protests and why many people devoted time and energy to saving it. And while such an account doesn't tell the whole story of the program's resurrection, it does tell an important one.

When they learned of the show's cancellation, fans began firing off letters to the station, composing petitions, and finally putting together a Facebook page—appropriately named Save A Place to Call Home or abbreviated as SAPTCH—to provide a framework for what was expected to be a long and sustained campaign aimed at convincing Channel 7 to reverse its decision. After four months of letters and petitions, fans received word that the show would go on because Foxtel, a streaming service, had ridden to its rescue. Once viewed as the essence of what constituted a lethal threat to local television production, a streaming platform set up an arrangement with Channel 7 that enabled the extraordinarily committed cast and crew to continue developing a narrative charged with significance. What Foxtel soon discovered from fans in the 140 countries with access to the program was that the Australian audience was hardly alone in its esteem for A Place to Call Home. Originally imagined as spanning three seasons, A Place To Call Home concluded its run at the end of its sixth year, yielding profits for the producers as well as prestige, and awards for the brilliant cast and the talented crew.

In an age that dismisses once celebrated social institutions like the family as purveyors of violence or of one or another evil, A Place To Call Home delved into the ways people can be both ground down but also built up by the relationships that structure their lives. As the personal testimonies included in this collection show, it took enormous courage to mobilize people and galvanize the energy to preserve the series. People had to be willing to engage publicly—many did so for the first time—and withstand the scrutiny and criticism that inevitably comes when voices are raised against the decision of a powerful institution. It took time and an attention to detail to ensure that the voices of the series' fans would be heard. This was an audacious undertaking by people from different professions and occupations who defied what were said to be strong market forces to preserve a story that gave meaning to their lives and to the world we all now inhabit. The moving accounts in this volume give some idea of what it took for men and women, not naturally disposed to protesting, to become comfortable with drawing public attention to their demands and to themselves. The stories also show how their joint actions magnified their shared trust and confidence in one another while forging friendships that continue to this day.

Taking advantage of Foxtel's decision to broadcast the program across the globe, the SAPTCHers as they are now known, then took the next step of helping to set up an international site to wire viewers in 140 countries into a circuit of skype chats with actors and writers even initiating essay contests to offer fans the chance to write—often with extraordinary eloquence--about a narrative they found fascinating and inspiring.

The role of social media and populism, said to be a toxic combination stoking prejudice and incivility, instead, became a catalyst for helping to preserve high quality culture and for bringing people together not only in Australia but also in countries across the globe. Over the years, the Skype chats with the creators, writers, and cast members deepened the attachment of people to the narrative, but also forged links among fans wherever they live. The Covid-19 era magnified the international exchanges with fans setting up Zoom meetings that include people from Australia, Europe, Israel, as well as from across the American continent. People talk not only about life under quarantine but also about aspects of a program now attracting a whole new cohort of viewers. Passionate Facebook discussions convinced people who might never have thought to travel to Australia to undertake the journey. Fans have also travelled from their homes to meet up in small gatherings in the United States and in England.

It was the Australians—Save A Place To Call Home [SAPTCH] founders—who established the pattern for social interactions. Aussies gathered together for picnics, parties, luncheons, and charity balls, some of these held on location at Camelot (aka Ash Park). They attended performances of cast members in theaters and bought tickets to their recitals in concert halls. They helped start fan clubs for the stars of the programs and informed people about their appearances and art exhibitions. SAPTCHers launched Facebook sites devoted to book recommendations and to Australian drama; some providing an encyclopedic list of films and television programs made in Australia.

Who are the fans? There are more women than men; many are teachers, while a high number are or were librarians and health care workers. Some have experience in theater or television production; some are retired from government service. When the program started to reach an international audience, the fans who participated in the Facebook discussions were spread out in 26 different countries in almost every part of the world.

The Australians who fought to preserve the series after it was cancelled may have been captivated both by its nostalgic restoration of a long-vanished world that once dazzled and commanded deference but also by its honest reckoning with the cruelty and prejudice wrought by its traditional decorum. The Facebook sites became forums for Australians to think about the experiences of their parents and grandparents during the decades when their country's social landscape was reshaped. Recognizing their own family ties to this story through memories of fashion, cars, architecture, music, cinema or even the China settings brought out of storage for special occasions, Australians imbued images of their past, once thought to be private and personal, with a new significance. Reclaiming their memories, Australians also recognized how much comfort they gave to their own uncertain times.

Discussions encouraged people to rethink their own assumptions and ask questions about stories of their families once deemed ordinary now understood as representing part of a social transformation that seemed boundless and therefore, also dangerous. How did it feel living with what was once thought to be a conventional and unshakeable a world view disappearing? How did their parents and grandparents prepare for what the future might bring when they had no way of knowing what it would be like when the world they knew dissolved? Facebook posts crackle with energy reflecting a general sense of people feeling as if they were standing at some sort of crossroad. The dialogues generate an atmosphere of spontaneity and the exhilarating feeling that the conversation could go anywhere. It sometimes does go off, simultaneously, in very different directions.

Facebook administrators monitor discussions to delete personal attacks, inappropriate comments, and even the occasional hacking, but never to stop people from expressing radically different views of plot or character. What episodes triggered the deepest sadness generated descriptions of suffering intended not to emphasize its uniqueness but rather to reveal it as part of the common human experience. Covid-19 quarantines created a new generation of ecstatic viewers who have pushed the virtual exchanges into something akin to communal gatherings not because of a common politics—in fact, no one much mentions their own ideological allegiances—but rather because of a shared interest in the narrative.

Because Covid-19 has surged its lethal microbes everywhere, intensifying dependence on social media, it might be helpful to consider the global connections A Place To Call Home Facebook sites generated if only to give some clarity to the idea of a world-event. The historical setting of the series encouraged people not only to think about the past, but also to recognize that the time in which we are living will someday be the past. Viewing the past from the present raises questions, but it also demands acts of imagination. It expands horizons if only because we now know that the traumas we could name or had heard of bled from one social class to another and from one decade to the next. And although the program is set in Australia, we, fans, from across the globe saw the story as belonging to our own world as well. That fans were drawn to travel to Australia was a natural outgrowth of wanting not only to see into a society once described as located at the end of the world but also to learn more about our own conflicts and about ourselves. Was this a unifying experience? Perhaps, not because we suddenly became one world wanting to erase the distinctiveness that comes from possessing a particular passport, but rather because we are more likely to see these differences as enriching rather than impoverishing life.

To say that the discussions have been spirited, then, is to downplay the vigor of the prose. Direct questions about plot receive widely divergent answers. Polls asking for fans to vote for their favorite character, love scene, or episode are hotly debated. Even questions about beloved dog, Lucky, can spark controversy. The only question some cannot answer is how many times the entire show or various seasons and episodes have been watched.

The energetic Facebook exchanges about characters, plot, and sex, allow people to see through these discussions the constraints that hem in life, the fractures within which we all live, and the compromises forged in the past that still haunt. But they also allow people to see how it may be possible to move forward. No character, no matter how limited the role, is exempted from comment. Even the most minor of characters animate discussion and disagreement—the working-class young tough for his violence and misogyny or the police for their easily manipulated prejudices. All of the exchanges prompt a rethinking of parochial assumptions about ethnic minorities but also about the individuals who hold so tightly to their biased views and are, perhaps, looking for markers of respect from the public realm. Fans recognize that A Place To Call Home speaks for a vanished world but in a vernacular that makes any observation of the past lead back to the present. Sarah Adams returns to her birthplace as almost a foreigner exiled from the cultural and social expectations imposed on her by family and community. This is a story of displacement that continuously draws people to see in it lessons for their own place and their own time.

Memory animates the narrative. In a country recovering from the wounds of war, the program shows how Australia regained its confidence by focusing on the lives of outcasts drawing together a subset of people living on the margins of society. The program does not get trapped in heavy handed social criticism; it focuses, instead on the practical particulars of people—their needs and their desires. It oscillates between love and passion, on the one hand, and social duty or familial responsibility, on the other. The mixture of longing and regret that makes up so much of life is interrogated, not bitterly or nostalgically, but candidly so that one story melts into another. The sheer talent of the actors convinces us that what we are seeing is not only plausible, but also absolutely true. What made the world inhabited by these men and women change is a theme whose significance has been recognized far beyond the geographic borders drawn in the series, perhaps, because the forces tearing people apart from one another are remarkably global. It is thus long past the time to give A Place To Call Home the tribute it so richly deserves as a story possessing an extraordinary power to draw people in and connect them to one another.

PART ONE: OUR STORIES
The Australians: Making History

PETER VERNON

I remember when the advertising for A Place to Call Home began. Mid 2012, Australia on the Seven Network. A new show was coming, a period piece and it looked phenomenal, unlike anything else I had seen on a commercial network before. I remember remarking to my wife Julie, that it looked really good and we should see what it was like. The teasers and trailers and ads continued for a good 6 months and the anticipation grew. Then finally the debut of the series in March 2013 and it was worth the wait. An Australian show, with a superb cast, brilliant writing and very obviously shot by an amazing crew. World class drama produced in our backyard. I was hooked. You have all seen the show and love it, so you know exactly what I mean. The ratings were through the roof, 1.4 million viewers per episode, which for Australia is phenomenal. It was Australia's highest rating drama for 2013. Season 2 was assured.

I remember thinking during the off season that there had not been the same publicity for Season 2. There was some but nowhere near as much as last year. It was pretty much "And now, here is Season 2 of A Place To Call Home" and there it was. Ok. I thought it was strange, but my favourite show was back and it was as good as last season. The ratings started to come through and it was still pulling an audience of around 900 000, which is still really solid for an Australian show, but not as good as last year. Each episode was amazing and the tension was building. Then the rumours started. The ratings weren't good enough for a show that cost over $1 000 000 per episode and Seven were considering their options, but the episodes continued. Then to my shock in June 2014 it was announced that APTCH had been axed. The episodes would continue, but an alternate ending had been shot and that would air. I couldn't believe it. The episodes continued and you could see the plot thickening and the season reaching a climax. The show was still incredible, and my anger at the axing grew. How could they do this.? An excellent show, still rating well despite the lack of publicity and they are axing it. I could not believe it. Each episode aired and I wondered how they would wrap it up with the ending it deserved. Plot lines were still building, the drama was escalating and you could see something big was going to happen. Then we made it to the final episode. I was hoping I would be satisfied with the end, still bitterly disappointed that the best show on TV was being axed. Throughout the episode we could see the tension build, something big was about to happen. You could just feel it and I kept wondering when does the wrap up start. Can't be long now, how are they going to tie this all up? Come on, start wrapping. Then it happened.

With two minutes to go, Rene smiles at Sarah, James and Olivia smile at each other cradling their beautiful baby seemingly happy, Elizabeth says her goodbyes and Norman drives her away, Regina looks smug and George walks in, he's visibly angry and storms out, Regina follows him and sees him ride off, she bursts into tears, but why? Can she sense their relationship is done with a look from George? We cut to the car driving away and the words "The End" flash up on the screen. That's it. Wow. I'm incredulous. Really. That's the ending. I was furious. What an absolutely atrocious way to treat the best show on TV.

Julie and I were very upset. But what could we do? Channel Seven was the biggest commercial network in Australia. They had made the decision and really what could we do. I sat thinking. Well, there is Change.org. The online petition site, maybe I could raise a petition. No. That won't work. 45- year- old men do not raise petitions to save TV shows. What would my friends say?

Next thing I knew, though I, was writing the petition. "A Place to Call Home is a world class Australian Drama with a sterling cast of actors. It's not often that a show like this comes along and it is rating solidly. Despite this the Seven Network has axed this show part way through season 2. I don't think there is any solid reason for this to happen. It is rating similarly to other dramas in the same timeslot, but Seven inexplicably have axed it……" I wrote. I continued on writing the rest of the petition. My hand hovered over the create button …. Do I really want to do this ….? "Oh fuck it" the thought came into my head and I hit the create button. It was done. The petition was live at https://www.change.org/p/the-seven-network-australia-save-a-place-to-call-home Done.

I watched the petition eagerly over the next few days. I posted the link on my Facebook Page. My friends, who were theatre lovers and very active in the arts were supportive. One of them had even had a speaking role in the show. 3 days in and I had 750 signatures. I'd also had a few messages. There were a few petitions raised and why was I raising another? I should close mine and help with the others. There was a big one raised by a young girl, I'd heard she was 15 or 16, who also loved the show. Em Johnson. It's interesting. Her petition has 10000 signatures now, mine has 7500. I tried to contact her via Facebook messenger, but I had no luck. No response. I wanted to see if we could work together to send Seven regular updates on our petitions. Sure they may have the same signatures, but I didn't think Channel Seven would ever really audit them to check. They'd assume there would be some crossover, but how much, who knows? Despite several attempts I never heard from her. Soon however the campaign would take a different turn.

I was on Facebook, actively sharing my petition amongst my friends, asking them to share it and I was commenting on a friend's post when I was tagged in the conversation. Some guy called Daniel Cooper. He was asking me if I was the Peter Vernon who had raised the petition to save APTCH. I looked at Daniel's profile. We had mutual friends, in fact some of my closest friends, so I responded that I was and sent him a friend request. Next thing I knew we were chatting. Dan, as I would soon come to call him, was an aspiring actor and loved the show too and he wanted to help. We brainstormed a bit and discovered we had a mutual friend in Paul Holmes, who had played the Church Of England Priest in the show - another friend with a speaking role. Paul is unfortunately no longer with us. (RIP Paul, you are missed.). We asked Paul if he knew of any way, we could do this and could he help. Paul was eager to see the show saved, but could only help from the wings, as if Seven got wind of his assistance it would mean it was highly unlikely he would work for them again. The industry is like that in Australia. You don't want to cross the networks. It is a career ending thing. I can't remember exactly who suggested it, but suddenly I was creating a Facebook Group called "Save A Place to Call Home" (SAPTCH) and a secret group called "Home Savers". Dan Paul and I were all in Home Savers, and this would be where we would discuss secret stuff. It didn't last long. Paul did not join SAPTCH but Dan and I were there. I would take the active role as leader, as I was not an aspiring actor and was prepared to give Seven hell. So was Dan, but it was much safer for me. I added the address for the group into the petition:

JUL 22, 2014 — "Hello Ladies and Gents, Wow the petition has hit over 5500 signatures. Well done all of you. I am so grateful for your support. I couldn't have done this without your generousity. I have sent a new copy of the petition to Seven and I am awaiting their response. I will let you know when I hear something.

On to the next stage of the campaign. We need to still share and support the petition so we get more signatures, but we have also created a Facebook group to support the great work we've done with the petition.

Head on over to https://www.facebook.com/groups/SAPTCH/ if you would like to join us in the next part of the campaign. Once again thanks for your support. I look forward to seeing you in the group. Cheers, Peter. "

As I am going back through links and things, other aspects of the campaign come to mind. There was also a Facebook Page, run by a guy called Trenton Goodwin. His page came before our group, but as It was a page it didn't work in the same way. It wasn't as interactive. Trenton would post something and people could comment, but unfortunately Seven would not see the comments on a Facebook page. Seven's social media was run by an external PR company and they would never convey any complaints or comments on an external page to Seven. We worked with Trenton to synchronise posts etc., and our membership grew from his page so his presence definitely helped us. I don't remember exactly what happened, but his page disappeared one day quite suddenly, but that was after the campaign had been won. I mention is though as it was a part of the campaign. We would share information we got from various sources, although there were aspects, we as a team kept close to our chests.

From this point on the petition would be a secondary part of the campaign. We didn't know it then, but Facebook and social media would turn out to be the key to saving the show. The beauty of the petition is that updates to it would go out to all the people that had signed the petition. As soon as I hit enter on the update the membership started to swell. From there, Dan and I started to rev up the members and continue to push the campaign and the petition. We still didn't know exactly what we were doing though. There were lots of discussions in the group and soon there were some stand out members. Jeni Lewington, an editor soon became an Admin. Imogen Crest who seemed to know quite a few people in theatre and TV circles became another one and the core team was formed.

We didn't do this alone though. Through friends of friends of friends I came across a contact who would help us immeasurably. An insider. I have mentioned Paul, but it wasn't him. There would be several people who would help us but this one was huge. A person who worked for Seven, and that's all I will ever say. Part of the reason we were successful is that people knew they could trust us as admins. We would never reveal who helped us from the inside and they knew that. Not unless they were happy for us to. Some were, some weren't. This person wasn't cast or crew, or a writer, but they knew how Seven worked. This person introduced me to " The Complaints Officer" Our weapon of choice. Under the Australian Television Code of Conduct, a commercial network has to provide an avenue for people to lodge complaints. For Seven that was "The Complaints Officer". When you wrote to the Complaints Officer, Seven had to reply to you, they had to table the complaint officially and they had to report the number of complaints to the Seven West Media Board. They didn't make it easy though. In the age of email and internet, you could not email them. No. You had to write a letter or send a fax. Ok. So be it. The campaign took a new direction. We would write letters. Lots of them. So the posts in the group became pleas to write letters. Little did we know how many letters would be generated. We heard that there was a stack of letters piled high at Seven, with Lizzies phone on top of it called Lizzies Complaint Line. Hilarious. More about the letters soon.

We did so many wonderful, innovative things to get our message out there. An absolute stroke of genius was our Sunrise Protest. August 12th, 2014. A really, really cold (by Sydney standard - yes us Aussies are freezing at temperatures most consider a balmy day) August morning set the stage for a protest in Sydney's Martin Place, the home of the studio of Seven's Morning Show "Sunrise". We got there at 6am just in time for the show to start. Daniel Cooper, Jeni Lewington, Jess Wales, Sue Southgate, Sandy Hodkinson, Annette Van Lierop and I all converged a on Sunrise to protest the axing. We had a huge banner made and Jess and Sandy had made signs for us to wave with the web address for the group, in the hope that we could use Seven's broadcast against them. Boy did it work. Have a look at https://tvtonight.com.au/2014/08/a-place-to-call-home-fans-in-sunrise-protest.html for pictures and details. We got our signs displayed and our membership grew. I still think that Sunrise was so supportive of us, because they could have easily kept us out of shot, but there we were several times, prominently displayed our signs clear and easy to read. Save A Place To Call Home. This protest would turn out to be a very inspiring day for us all. I remember it fondly and am very glad I got up at 3am to travel by train to Sydney. Thanks to TV tonight for their support ,too. Media coverage of any kind was very hard to get. Seven was a big advertiser for all of the major papers, so getting them to support us was impossible. We did however get some media support along the way:

https://www.dailytelegraph.com.au/newslocal/macarthur/fans-of-a-place-to-call-home-are-pleadi ng-for-channel-7-to-bring-it-back-for-a-third-season/news-story/8a8097a1bd5e8b85581b4ed557 1008a7

https://www.dailymercury.com.au/news/angry-tv-fans-petition-seven-over-place-call-home-/2340 962/

I said I would mention more about the letters. They were absolutely key to our success. Throughout the campaign we heard lots of reasons as to why APTCH was axed. One of them was how expensive the show was to produce, $800 000 to $1 000 000 per episode and the demographic it skewed to was mainly over 45, which is not the magic audience. The magic audience is 18 - 45. Apparently that demographic is pliable and open to suggestions from advertisers. The rest of us are apparently so stuck in our ways and not worth much to Woolworths, Coles or Bunnings (major Australian retailers). The funny thing is we found that the audience was so much wider than they thought, from 10 to 87. Families watched the show together. Parents and grandparents discussed it with kids. It was a very widely aged viewership. The thing with an older demographic though is they love to write letters. Hundreds of them in fact.

Thousands. We would have letter writing campaigns. Each week I would put up a post for our target for the letters, so this week we are writing to Tim Worner and Tim would receive a few hundred letters. The next week it was Julie McGauran and so on. People would write to the highlighted person and they would also write to the Complaints officer. We heard they were so overwhelmed that they could not respond to us all. I never received a response to my letters, but others did. Not many though.

To help people write to Seven, people like Bridget McNamara wrote form letters that people could print out and sign. Anne Seacombe printed Business cards and Postcards via vista print that people could sign and mail in. We had files on our site that people could download and send. We also had paper petitions.

Another method we could use was fax, but who has a fax machine though? I discovered that you could send a fax via the internet, and so I posted details on the group of the site, and a letter that people could enter into the page to fax to Seven. Within a week or so the site was onto us, and the number for Seven was blocked, so we found a few more services we could use until they blocked us. Sorry to those services for the 'misuse' but thanks for helping us in our mission to bombard Seven.

Every time the petition hit another 1000 signatures, I would print it out and mail it to Seven. I did that 8 times.

Social media was a key part of the campaign too and we used Seven's social media against them. Seven decided in their wisdom to release a DVD of season 2 and they posted about it on their Facebook page. They may have made some DVD sales from it, though I am not sure how many!! What it did get them for their trouble though was thousands and thousands of angry comments from people about them axing the show. All of these people were Facebook users and they were furious. It gave me the perfect way to recruit members who would be happy to write letters. I spent hours replying to as many comments as possible, to give them the address for the group and ask them to join the group fighting to save the show. We got so many letter writing members from that.

We were on Twitter as well. Lots of angry fans were there too, berating Seven for axing the show. Each one of them got a response from one of us asking them to join the group. We had to make each tweet slightly different so that Twitter would not reject it. Using someone's twitter handle in the message helped.

Sometimes our own group would work against us though, or at least the things they heard and shared. It was never intentional, just some of the news would affect morale. Every now and then someone would post telling us we were all wasting our time as the show was never coming back. I remember one post that announced that all the sets had been destroyed, the cars had been sold, the costumes were sold and all the props were gone. We already knew this of course. We had a lot of information on what was happening. Dan and I were Musical Theatre people and a lot of TV sets are sold off to Theatre companies and they use them for sets in their productions. After a quick brainstorm we responded saying that the sets were at a local theatre company and that all of the props were still available and the cars were easy to access. Phew. Crisis averted. When Foxtel saved the show, they ended up having to recreate all the sets. Seven had indeed destroyed them so that another network could not use the sets and resurrect the show.

When I saw the sets, I was amazed at how sturdy they were. Each archway and doorway in the Ash Park set was so solid. The walls were high but there was no ceiling as all the lighting was suspended above. The exterior walls were open stud walls but they did not move. Interestingly when then show was axed, Roy's Farmhouse at Camden was completely gutted and renovated. It looked the same outside, but the inside was now modern, so it could not be used for shooting except for the exterior. Foxtel solved this issue by recreating Roy's house in full in a studio in Sydney. It was incredibly detailed.

Our leadership was often challenged as well. Early on, we had a tech guy with whom there was a falling out. I got many messages from people calling me an idiot and telling me I had no idea what I was doing. Ok. Thanks. I deleted and moved on. I remember one person who was telling me the direction I was taking us on was just completely wrong. I was on a family holiday when they insisted I take their advice many times. I would message them back on breaks in driving, and they would reply telling me how foolish I was. I smiled at the messages as I knew that in the background, we were incredibly close to the show being saved. We played a lot of our cards close to our chests, we had to, in order to save the show. If people got wind that we knew what was happening it would be disastrous.

I remember hearing the news when we were successful, when all was sorted and the show was saved. We had been planning for a while to hold a nationwide series of picnics to protest the axing of the show, thinking if it was big enough and had a fun angle that we would possibly get some media coverage. We had invited some cast, hoping they would come and maybe that was how word got back, but next thing I knew I had the lovely Vanessa Hollins from Foxtel on the phone asking me if they could assist us with the organisation of the picnics and perhaps bring some cast along. Of course they could!! That was the moment I knew that we had won. What a moment that was. It was a relatively short campaign, around 3-4 months of lots of work and constant pestering of Seven, but it showed Foxtel that there was a readymade audience for this amazing show.

The party we had at Observatory Hill was amazing. Foxtel brought us food and drink and cast members! Another surreal moment when Noni walked up and she knew who I was. Her hugs are the best, by the way. Nothing like a Noni hug. Meeting Marta and Ben. She brought her kids and my boys played with her girls. Meeting the lovely Sara Wiseman who spoke with a Kiwi accent rather than her absolutely perfect Aussie accent in the show. Then meeting Arianwen who in real life has a lovely Aussie accent and doesn't sound like an English rose. The lovely Jenni Baird who is so sweet and kind, and nothing at all like Regina. The amazing Aldo. They were with us for a few hours and were so gracious and kind. They spoke to people all over the country and the world via skype including Natalie Fainstein in Jerusalem, Anne Seacombe in Tasmania. Brett and Craig were in Melbourne for the picnic there and Brian Walsh went to Camden to meet the SAPTCHERs there. It was an amazing day. One I will never forget.

Then there was the Premiere of Season 3 in North Sydney where I met Abby Earl, but it went along the lines of her exclaiming "Oh my god, you're Peter Vernon!!" Umm. Yes, and you are the amazing Abby Earl. Then there was David Berry greeting me on set for S3 and the Inverness Town scene where George announces he is running for Parliament.

Then there were articles about our success.

An interview I did with Joy FM when we were successful: https://joy.org.au/murphyslaw/2014/10/interview-with-peter-vernon-save-a-place-to-call-home/

https://www.couriermail.com.au/news/queensland/a-place-to-call-home-may-have-found-new-ne twork-after-it-was-dumped-by-channel-seven/news-story

https://www.smh.com.au/entertainment/tv-and-radio/new-home-for-a-place-to-call-home-201410 14-115u4c.html

https://www.news.com.au/entertainment/tv/the-miraculous-story-of-how-people-power-saved-tel evision-drama-a-place-to-call-home/news-story/ff71a99d987221293d1d3ff9da1bbf31

From there the adventure had only just begun. Foxtel hosted us at Garden Parties. Dan and I became regular extras on the show. Over the course of the campaign I had become friends with Noni and I emailed her asking if there was any chance, we could be extras on the show. The next thing I know my phone rings and it is Noni. The extras casting director will be calling me to get details of names and then for us to fill out the appropriate forms etc. Suddenly, Dan, Jeni, Julie and I are on the set of A Place To Call Home on the first day of filming for Season 3 Episode 1. It was meant to be day 14, but the weather caused them to bring forward the filming of internal scenes and so we were there when the very first scene of Season 3 was shot. It was meant to be, I think. I will never forget the first scene I was in. I was standing in front of Dr Jack Duncan's office door, and in the office standing right in front of me was Marta dressed as Sister Sarah Adams. I was trying not to look at her, but also drawn to look at her. I couldn't believe my eyes. She looked up and saw me looking and I smiled. It would have been a very big smile. I just couldn't believe it. She smiled back and winked at me. Wow. Just wow. Then the director called action and she became Sarah and walked past me. I will never forget it.

The other wonderful thing that happened that day was that Noni came in to have lunch with us. She wasn't on set that day but she made the trip especially to see us. When you are on set, catering is provided and it is lovely food. I remember getting my plate together and talking to Noni all through lunch, but not eating much. One of the assistant directors came over and said to Noni that she could take us through the sets and we jumped at the chance. We were only shooting at the hospital that day, so the other sets were closed, but Noni got us into them. As we walked through the recreation of Ash Park, I was truly amazed at the detail. Old federation houses are sturdy. I have been to Camelot/Ash Park in real life, and the door frames are about 30cm thick. The door frames on the set were the same, so thick and sturdy. The walls on the outside were open stud walls, but the insides were beautifully decorated with period wallpaper and the murals we saw on the show. Huge tall ceilings but no actual ceiling just row after row of lights. The outside of the walls looked like they would move if the doors were closed, but Noni showed us. Those walls did not move. These were the second version of the sets. The original sets were destroyed and Foxtel/Seven had built them all again. The workmanship was incredible. You felt transported.

The detail in all the sets was incredible. The government health signs in the hospital. The magazines on the tables were authentic. The furniture and knick-knacks added to the authenticity. When dressed in your costume you felt like you had time travelled.

Noni also took us into the newly created interior of Roy's house. In the hiatus between the show being cancelled and reinstated , the people that owned Roy's real farmhouse had used the money they got for its use to fully gut and renovate the inside. Gone was the rustic farmhouse. Now there was a new home with high end kitchen appliances and a modern look. Luckily, they had not gotten to the exterior so it could still be used from the outside, but the inside needed to be recreated and so there it was in the middle of a big warehouse in the inner west of Sydney. It was perfect.

Funny story. When we came back from our tour dessert had been served. In my rush to visit the set I had left my barely eaten lunch, too busy talking to Noni, and there it was, the only plate left at the many tables where we had eaten. You clear your own plate of course. I went to go to attend to it only to have Noni insist she would do it, that I should get some dessert while it was there. I said that it was fine I would take care of it, but Noni was insistent. It was a surreal moment, Noni Hazlehurst - legend of the Australian entertainment industry clearing my plate that I had left when I shouldn't have. I have to say, that's Noni to a tee. There would be other occasions on set where she would look after us, always saving us a seat at her table. She is a wonderful, caring person.

It was always incredible to see the process of how an episode was made. I did a very memorable 3-day shoot at Manly for the episode where Sarah sees the German woman who tormented her in the concentration camp. It was at Manly Heads, and over 3 days I think I worked 27 hours over the 3 days. 4am starts, 8 pm finishes. A lot of it waiting around but wonderful to see Brett and Marta working their craft. I was at a 2-day shoot for the Douglas Goddard Memorial fund with Noni, Sara, Craig, Arianwen, Abby, Tim, Brett and Marta all on set. I saw Noni do many takes of her speech in that scene. The shoot it from different angles and perspectives. Her absolute consistency was amazing. The same inflection here, the pause there. It's a joy to watch. Shooting inside Swifts, which is the Swanson Mansion. I did another 3 day shoot there and at the end you see my back walking into the house and me smoking a Hookah pipe which was a vaping pen taped to the nozzle of the pipe. I had to blow the 'smoke' high into the air but being steam it was hard to get the desired effect. We got it after many goes. I hope that stuff is safe!! All part of the fun. It was the bohemian scene when Caro kisses Delia. I knew something big was happening that day. I was there in the corner watching as Jack catches them and storms out. It was a great scene. I spent 3 cold wet winter days in trousers, a cotton shirt, a cravat and a smoking jacket. I did better than some of the ladies though. We suffer for our art. Lol. I could have been at Carolyn and Jacks wedding as one of their Sydney guests. Unfortunately, I couldn't get there. I still regret that, but I had lots of great experiences. My last shoot was the last official extras shoot, when Anna and Olivia attend court. We were at the Balmain Courthouse and when Arianwen saw me we hugged and had a chat. She asked me who I was playing for the day and I said I was a barrister apparently. She had a brilliant idea, I would be her barrister, I was already walking behind her in the scene we were shooting and she said to the director that it would feel better for her if she turned around and shook my hand before she runs into Anna. The director agreed and so we shot that scene a few different ways. I didn't say anything, as that would involve me being paid more and that couldn't happen, but she did shake my hand and thank me. Unfortunately, it didn't make it to the final cut but it was fun to shoot and great of Arianwen to do that for me. It was the last official extras day. I was there for the first and last days of the shooting of the show we saved. I feel so lucky. To think they actually paid me for it. I would have done it for free!!

There is so much to the last 4 years of A Place To Call Home. Dinner dances, galas, picnics, parties, friendships but most of all the community. Two Facebook groups of people from all over the world who love the show and now know each other. That's really the best part. The community and connections that have been formed. The friendships that will last for life, all formed because Seven along with Bevan Lee created a masterpiece of a show. Then they axed it and we responded. A Place to Call Home is now seen in over 144 countries and universally acclaimed and loved. I would actually like to thank Seven for axing the show, almost as much as I would like to thank Foxtel for saving it. If that hadn't happened, nothing that followed would have happened. This campaign changed my life and many other lives. Our wonderful show went from a possible 3 seasons to an actual 6 seasons. It was treated with the utmost respect and care it always deserved. I made wonderful friends from the cast, crew and group, people I will be friends with for life. On top of all that I saw the end of "The End" in season 2, and the proper ending of the show that we always deserved. I can't tell you how proud I was to see that ending. How the tears rolled as we saw how each of the characters ended up. The friends we lost, the lives lived to the full, Henry and Harry marrying. It was so satisfying.

There are so many things I haven't covered here and I can't and have this be a decent length. Hopefully others will recount them in their words and from their experiences. It has been an amazing ride. I would not change a moment of it. The fact that we saved the show is one of my proudest moments. That I was able to start the campaign and lead it an absolute honour. Thank you to everyone that joined us. Thank you for all you did to make yourself heard. We were quite the force. We made television history. The second show in Australian television history to be saved, Neighbours was the first when it went from Seven, yes Seven, to Network 10 and then A Place to Call Home that went from Seven to Seven/Foxtel. So many people told us it would never happen. Thank the universe we didn't listen. I am so grateful for A Place to Call Home. It is the show that has changed all our lives.

MY SAPTCHER JOURNEY
JENI LEWINGTON

Where to start? I have so many wonderful memories from the last six years that it's hard to focus on just one or two themes so I'm going to try to encapsulate them all.

It all began when season two of A Place To Call Home (APTCH) ended abruptly with that now famous 'The End' episode. There has to be more to the show than that, I thought. I was angry that Channel 7 had treated this incredible show with such disdain and I immediately created a Facebook page called Channel 7 Don't Axe A Place to Call Home, which became A Place To Call Home is Saved in late 2014 following the Foxtel/Channel 7 deal.

Timeline of major events

• 28 April 2013	Season 1 premiered
• 11 May to 13 July 2014	Season 2 premiered
• 18 July 2014	Peter Vernon [PV] created The "Save A Place To Call Home" Group
• 19 July 2014	PV added admin Daniel Cooper [DC]
• 20 July 2014	DC added admins Imogen Crest [IC] and Jeni Lewington [JL]
• 31 July 2014	JL added Noni Hazlehurst
• 12 August 2014	Sunrise protest
• 26 October 2014	Celebratory picnics
• 20 April 2015	First day of filming Season 3
• 25 August 2015	Foxtel TV special with the cast of APTCH
• 5 September 2015	Garden party, Camelot
• 27 September 2015	Season 3 premiered
• 22 May 2016	Nielson Café lunch attended by cast members.
• 6 September 2016	Foxtel BBQ, Camelot

- 11 September 2016   Season 4 premiered
- 11 March 2017   Dinner dance, Camelot
- 11/12 March 2017   Location tours
- 23 April 2017   APTCH wins Logie for Most Outstanding Drama Series
- 8 October 2017   Season 5 premiered
- 13 October 2018   Gala fundraiser, Camelot
- 13/14 October 2018   Location tours
- 19 August 2018   Season 6 premiered
- 2019   Frankie J Holden wins Logie for Most Outstanding Supporting Actor

I can't remember exactly when I discovered Peter Vernon's petition, but pretty soon after I, along with Peter, Daniel Cooper and Imogen Crest, were administrators on The "Save A Place To Call Home" Facebook Group that Peter had set up on 18 July 2014 and from then on we were Busy (with a capital B) adding new members, encouraging members to write letters to Channel 7, getting Save APTCH T-shirts printed and distributed, organising a very successful protest outside Channel 7's morning TV show, Sunrise, on the 12 August 2014, and coordinating media releases and protest picnics (which turned out to be celebratory picnics) in Australia and around the world on 26 October 2014.

I remember joining up one member in particular very early in our campaign, Noni Hazlehurst, on 31 July 2014. It was extremely exciting to have cast members joining us knowing that they were as passionate about the show as all of us were.

Sunrise protest and early media coverage

Things moved quickly during July and August 2014. On 11 August I flew from Brisbane, Queensland, to Sydney and stayed with another fan, Sandy Hodkinson, overnight. On 12 August we got up very early to catch a taxi to the Sunrise studio to meet up with other fans of the show. It was fantastic to meet everyone for the first time.

L to R in photo: Peter Vernon, Chris McClennan, Jeni Lewington, Sue Southgate, Jess Wales, Sandy Hodkinson, Daniel Cooper and Annette Van Lierop

Decked out in our Save A Place To Call Home T-shirts, we braved the cold and rain on what turned out to be the coldest Sydney day on record. We were able to get our message across to Channel 7 very well, which was matched with a Twitter campaign from fans watching at home.

In Brisbane, we got some newspaper coverage in The Courier Mail.

L to R: Trenton Goodwin, Jeni Lewington, Phillipa Pender, Dawn Trethaway

Opportunities to visit the locations

After the success of our Sunrise protest, I visited the Argyle Steps before travelling to Camden the following day to stay with Sammy Nilsson, her husband Patrick, and their daughter Victoria for a couple of nights in order to visit some of the filming locations that are in the area and we also arranged to get interviewed by a couple of local newspapers outside the Camelot gates.

Sammy met me at the train at 10.30 am on 13 August and we joined Jess Wales, Judy Grech and Catherine Matic at Camelot at 11 am where we were met by Brian from The Macarthur Chronicle for a photo shoot. After an hour we went to Cobbity Church, which was used as the Bligh church. We shared information about our cause with random passersby and used the church noticeboard to share our postcards/petition etc.

After lunch, where we again brochure-bombed the café we ate at, it was back to Camelot for 2 pm to meet Lee, from The Post Reporter. Amazingly, after the interview, Catherine started chatting to a lady doing the whipper-snippering and discovered she was the owner of Camelot, Rachel! We got a great insight into the production of APTCH. Apparently, the house is registered with seven production agencies and it was used in the film Australia too.

L to R: Jess Wales, Jeni Lewington, Sammy and Victoria Nilsson, Judy Grech, Catherine Matic outside the gates of Camelot

Rachel wasn't aware of our campaign, so we gave her some postcards and business cards. She mentioned she knew people at Channel 7 and that she would speak to them about us, which was fantastic news! She also confirmed that two endings had been shot and that the cast only found out late that this was happening. She said the cast were as disappointed as us and wanted it to continue.

Anyway, after that serendipitous meeting, Jess, Judy and Catherine had to go, but Sammy, Victoria and I continued on to St James' Anglican Church, Menangle, where Anna and Gino got married. The church wasn't open, but we tracked down a lovely lady, Ros, who had the keys and let us inside. We left a petition, business cards and postcards because Ros said many people would want to sign.

The day APTCH was saved

Sunday 26 October 2014 will forever be etched on our minds. After a four-month campaign writing copious letters, signing petitions, having newspaper articles written about us, making T-shirts, developing a website and standing outside the Sunrise studios on the coldest day of the year, we found out for certain that APTCH had been saved by a partnership between Foxtel and Channel 7 and two more seasons would be made.

We had originally planned the 26 October as a day of protest, but it turned into a wonderful celebration across Australia and indeed the world. Part of my role was to coordinate the picnics and prepare media releases. As well as seventeen 1950s-inspired picnics held simultaneously in every state and territory in Australia, overseas representatives from Germany, the US, the UK and Israel also participated.

Inspired by the show, we all donned 1950s outfits and enjoyed meeting people we had only met previously online via Facebook, brought together by our shared love of APTCH. People who couldn't be at a picnic sent selfies of themselves from wherever they were (e.g. on holiday in South Korea, even on a cruise).

Cast members turned up to the Melbourne and Sydney picnics and we arranged some Skype calls to other picnics, in Australia and overseas. This was the first time I spoke with Noni, Arianwen and Jenni from the Sydney picnic. Foxtel CEO Brian Walsh turned up to the Camden picnic. We even coined a new term for ourselves: SAPTCHers (Save A Place To Call Homers].

After our picnics, we displayed changing Facebook banners every couple of days to acknowledge all the people who had contributed to our campaign.

On location with APTCH: A day in the life of an extra

Who wouldn't jump at the chance to be an extra on your favourite show?

On Monday 20 April 2015 (which just happened to be the very first day of filming for season 3), I, along with fellow "Save A Place to Call Home Group" admins (Peter Vernon, Daniel Cooper) and fans (Julie Vernon, Sandy Hodkinson), were privileged to be given the opportunity to be extras for a day by way of a thank you from Noni Hazlehurst for helping to resurrect the show. It was wonderful to meet some of the cast (Marta Dusseldorp, Brett Climo, Craig Hall, Deborah Kennedy, Frankie J Holden and Noni Hazlehurst) and crew, who were all very appreciative of our efforts and excited to be back on set for another season.

Prior to filming day, we were told what parts we would play and were given instructions to bring along any 1950s-inspired clothes to assist wardrobe. Sandy and I were to be patients in Inverness Hospital, while Peter, Daniel and Julie were visitors. We were going to be on set in the Sydney studios! I could hardly wait.

On Sunday 19 April, I flew (at my own expense) to Sydney from Brisbane and was picked up by my cousin, Barbara Hutchins, who I would be staying with. At 5.30 am on Monday 20 April, my cousin and I arrived at the Sydney studios. We were issued with a call sheet, which sets out all the crew contact and arrival details, the specific scenes to be shot, props required etc. There was even a lovely message on the back of the call sheet that read:

We would like to welcome some of the Admin Team from 'The Save A Place To Call Home Group' who are extras with us today.

First stop until 6.45 AM was hair and makeup courtesy of Cassie Hanlon. The first thing I noticed was a big trailer next to the hair and makeup tables and who should emerge not long after I sat down but Marta Dusseldorp. After hair and makeup, it was onto wardrobe where the lovely Jacqui ensured Sandy and I were kitted up in nighties, dressing gowns, slippers; Peter and Dan got their suits and hats, and Julie got her gloves etc. It was amazing to see the rows of clothes and boxes of shoes all numbered neatly. Walking to wardrobe we passed the props area, a vast expanse of all things 1950s. After wardrobe, I actually went back to makeup to get the tattoo on my left wrist hidden with makeup (not the done thing for a young 1950s woman to have!). While I was there, Wizzy Molineux put a couple more rollers in my hair. It was really interesting hearing about all the productions Wizzy and Cassie had worked on.

Breakfast, from 6.45 to 7.15 am, was a sumptuous buffet feast with an array of hot and cold food. It was surreal to be in line behind Brett Climo! We were all spruced up and ready for action, but we had a bit of a wait to go on set so hung around in the lunchroom.

After a lot of waiting around finally it was my big moment – playing a patient with Peter (my pretend husband) visiting me in hospital for some unknown complaint. My heart was beating furiously. First hurdle was to get into the bed because it was old and high. This was achieved with the aid of a stepladder. Then the call 'All quiet on set' as the actors went through their paces two or three times before they called a wrap on that scene. One interesting anecdote is Peter had to smoke pretend [herbal] cigarettes in keeping with the times.

From 12.30 to 1.15 pm it was lunch and Noni joined us especially even though she was not filming that day. There was a welcome cacophony of sound in the lunchroom. After lunch Noni gave us a tour around the studio where we saw the internal areas of Inverness Hospital, Ash Park and Roy's house.

Opportunities to meet the cast (2014-2020)

From the first picnic, when cast members Skyped us in Brisbane, to being an extra and the Foxtel TV special, to attending the screen premieres of Seasons 3/4/5 and 6, various events at Camelot, the Logies and the AACTA awards, as well as attending cast theatre projects post APTCH, I've met most of the cast at one time or another.

The Foxtel cast TV special was the first time many fans got to meet cast members en masse. It was a fantastic night and was held just before the screening of Season 3.

Foxtel TV special

So far, we have had four major events at Camelot [aka Ash Park] – a BBQ, a garden party, and two dinner dances.

Camelot Garden Party 2015

I have attended three Logies events – one in Melbourne in 2016, and two on the Gold Coast in 2018 and 2019. The 2018 one was the best because a lot of the cast were there, it was just after my birthday and every cast member wished me a happy birthday. I was on cloud nine for days!

Logies 2018

It is not only APTCH that has inspired fans, but also any theatre projects of cast members post-APTCH, so I have attended plays in Sydney starring Sara Wiseman, Mark Lee and Tim Draxl, a variety performance by Frankie J Holden and his wife Michelle Pettigrove, plays in Melbourne, Hobart and Brisbane starring Marta Dusseldorp and Ben Winspear, and I've seen Noni Hazlehurst in her one-woman play Mother at least five times.

Friendships forged worldwide

Throughout the six years I have made friends with fans from Australia and around the world in Israel, the USA, the UK, the Netherlands and Singapore, and have had the pleasure of sharing filming locations with visitors from overseas, including Gail Seigel [Israel], Donna Robinson Divine and Jane Gordon Sullivan [USA], Fran Simmons [UK], Marjolein Hul and Nell Van de Graaf [Netherlands].

A variety of subgroups have been formed focusing on, for example, recipes, books, arts and crafts, and Australian film, TV and theatre. In addition, individual fan pages have been created for cast members (e.g. Marta Dusseldorp, Brett Climo, Craig Hall, Sara Wiseman, Noni Hazlehurst, Jack Ellis, Frankie J Holden and David Berry).

Along the way, we have sadly had to say farewell to members who have passed away in the last six years. They include Andy Munro, Sue Notary, Daniel Cooper's parents, Rosemary and Robert Cooper, Kate Harding, Shirley Pollard, Pauline and Neville Grove [aka Dick and Dora]. as well as Paul Holmes, who played Reverend Green on APTCH.

And yet we have also welcomed many new babies into the SAPTCHer family from cast members as well as fans. Abby Earl and her partner welcomed twins in 2020, David Berry and his wife welcomed a boy around 2016, while fans Sam and Colleen Piantodosi had a girl in 2018, and Kimba Green and her husband Russell had a girl, River, in 2017 and another girl, Summer, in 2020.

I love APTCH so much, I wrote a book

I think from the first trip I made to Sydney and Camden, and from being an extra on set, I was intrigued about the filming locations, and these experiences planted the seed that got me thinking about writing a book on the filming locations from APTCH. In our groups we had avid fans who were fixated on discovering the locations and it was exciting to try to figure out where different scenes had been filmed.

As I wanted to do the right thing by all the locations, I consulted an intellectual property lawyer in the first instance who helped me draft a permission form to send to all the locations that we knew about. This proved to be a tricky process because a couple of locations did not want their whereabouts to be known. Eventually I designed privacy icons that indicated whether a property was open to the public or not and negotiated with locations about which details they wanted in the book. This inevitably meant that only one location refused to be mentioned in the book at all, so in the end we had 30 filming locations in total--10 from Camden and 20 from Sydney.

Next, I had to travel to each of the locations to take photos, because I wasn't permitted under copyright to use any of Channel 7's photos. This involved at least two trips to Sydney from Brisbane and the assistance of various fans for accommodation and transport who are all acknowledged in my book. I also engaged a graphic designer to create 30 individual maps and two large area maps for the locations. Research involved about six months of library and internet research to find out the history of each location.

Finally, in mid-2016 my book, called Jeni's APTCH Location Guidebook, was published and all 600 copies were either gifted to cast members or given to people who had contributed to my GoFundMe campaign. An eBook version was also produced, which is still available, and the only way to get a hard copy now is via print-on-demand from Amazon's US shop.

Facebook post from 6 July 2018

And so, the curtain falls for the last time on our beloved show and I'd just like to take a few moments to post my thanks to a few people.

First, thanks to Peter Vernon, Daniel Cooper and Imogen Crest for being the best co-admins I could wish for. We haven't always seen eye-to-eye, but we have been able to discuss our different perspectives and have been through a lot together in the past four years, from our first meeting on 14 August 2014 at our Sunrise protest. I look forward to maintaining the group with you all.

Next, to Vanessa Hollins thank you for your behind-the-scenes efforts to support all us SAPTCHers, especially at the Logies, and listening when I asked if it might be possible to organise set visits for our international fans Gail Siegel, Jane Gordon Sullivan and Donna Robinson Divine.

To the many friends I've met through the group from Sydney, Melbourne, Perth, Adelaide, Canberra, Alice Springs, thanks for your friendships, which I'm sure will endure.

A few special thank yours go to Alice Child who hosted me in Alice Springs last year, friends who have hosted me in Sydney and Camden (Sandy Hodkinson, Sammy Nilsson, Brenda Fowler, Anne Kimber, Lyndal Spencer, Donna Robertson), and friends who helped distribute my book (Dolores Ryan, Jane Wiles, Karyn Pagano, Margaret Jackson, Jess Wales, Peter Vernon, Daniel Cooper, Kerrie Marr. Rachel Anne, Katrina Hayes, and my parents John and Margaret Lewington). A big thank you to the location owners for opening up their homes/hospitals/offices etc.

Thanks to Channel 7 for cancelling the show, the impetus for us to come together. Thanks to Foxtel and Brian Walsh for giving us four more seasons. Thanks to Noni Hazlehurst for giving me the opportunity to be an extra in season 3 episode 2. Thanks to all the cast and crew for your superb work. Finally, thanks to Bevan Lee, the maestro behind the words.

#farewellAPTCH #APTCHalwaysinourhearts

A Place to Call Home fans in Sunrise protest

August 13th, 2014, By David Knox comments Filed under: News,

Aggrieved fans of **A Place to Call Home** took to Martin Place yesterday to let **Sunrise** and Channel Seven know what they think of axing the period drama.

Rain did not deter the fans, aged 21-60, some of whom have set up a new website at saptch.com with links to social media resources and petitions.

So far there are 3 petitions totaling almost 18,000 signatures.

Webmaster Peter Vernon told **TV Tonight**, "We created the website to provide a landing page and web presence that gave us an easy way to get people involved in the campaign to Save **A Place To Call Home**.

"The site provides details for each avenue available within the campaign, including Facebook, Twitter and Petitions – both online and paper and gives us a simple, easy to remember address that people can go to. It also lets people find out what's happening with the campaign via our blog and media contacts as the campaign is gaining more recognition in the media.

"If people are not on Facebook or Twitter there's also details on who you can write to at Seven. It's basically a one stop shop for saving **A Place to Call Home**."

In Camden where the series filmed exteriors, even the local bank has taken opportunity telling customers, "It's OK Camden. We can help you find another place to call home with a great home loan from NAB."

Hovering above the words is an axe….

Photo: Brett Atkins

Share this:

A little reminder to all SAPTCHers that small catch-ups with fellow members can be marvelous occasions without the need for an organised event! I have met many wonderful people through just connecting with our community and mutual interests. Reach out ... Today I met up with

Alison Apps

and

Jeni Robinson

for a lunch date which had a few schedule changes ('cos we're all busy) ... Such a fabulous afternoon of friendship, sharing stories of our lives (and some 6 degrees of separation). And guess what? We didn't talk about APTCH, because that common denominator was a given. Engage, I say!

79Margaret Jackson, Bridget McNamara and 77 others

26 Comments

Jenni Goodwin

Author

For the international members ... the headland above Ally's head (on the left) is Cape Byron, which is the most easterly point on the Australian mainland. Just saying ... 🙂

DOLORES RYAN

I remember it vividly-- the first day that APTCH was to air on Channel 7. After weeks of advertising and much anticipation, and excitement, the day had finally arrived.

It was a family day, and my Mother-in Law was spending the day with us. She too was looking forward to seeing the first episode at her home that evening. We talked about it for quite some time, even though we hadn't seen a single episode yet, talking about what we hoped it would be like and how it was going to be wonderful to have a lovely period drama to watch instead of reality television.

We had intended to have a post episode discussion, but sadly that wasn't to be, as my Mother-In-Law, Joan passed away 2 days later. That Sunday was the last time we would see her. I never got to find out what her thoughts were about APTCH, but without a doubt I'm sure she absolutely loved it as much as I did. As the series went on, I said to my husband, numerous times, "Your Mum would have loved this show".

As the episodes went on my family became very familiar with it being a "Do Not Disturb" time and left me alone to enjoy what had become my favourite series of all time.

Fast forward to the end of Season 2 and I was absolutely mortified and in total disbelief that Channel 7 had planned to axe the series. WHY, WHY, WHY!!!!!

Those feelings soon turned to complete anger and I was so bloody furious after watching the final episode. How the hell could they disrespect the fans so much to have given the series such a disgusting and unbelievable Finale? I was totally gob smacked!!!

I was so angry I had a major rant, yelling as I stomped through the house saying things like "How could they do that", "Do they think we're morons", "Are we supposed to believe that crap ending" "How Bloody Stupid", etc., etc., etc. My poor family didn't know what was going on but they were very sympathetic, as they knew how important APTCH had become to me.........they hadn't seen just how so at this point but they soon would.

Not too long after the series had ended my Husband, Rob, was reading the paper and saw a small article regarding APTCH and how a Facebook group had been formed to save the series. More proof as to how much I loved the show as Rob doesn't always take notice of what my interests are, but he certainly took notice of this one. Ha-ha!!! I wish I had kept that article but I didn't realise at the time just how important it would become to me.

I immediately joined "The Save A Place To Call Home" group and have been forever grateful to my Husband for bringing it to my attention. Joining up so early in the piece allowed me to fully embrace the fight and, along with countless others, constantly send letters to Channel 7 to help save the series.

Fast forward again to the protest picnics that were being organised around the country. I couldn't attend that day but I was glued to my iPad to see all the posts, photos and comments from all the other SAPTCHers who were attending.

Imagine my surprise when I found that the protest became a victory and that Foxtel was going to pick up the series. It was actually announced that morning in the Sunday paper and my delight and excitement was immeasurable, and I have a special photo of me with the article as a memento. Seeing all the photos coming through with cast members, APTCH postcards, Foxtel APTCH cupcakes etc. was absolutely amazing and I was so overjoyed I remember crying with happiness. Foxtel certainly nailed the surprise element that day. IT'S A DAY I WILL NEVER, EVER FORGET, even though I couldn't be at the picnic in person to enjoy it.

This was the beginning of a truly wonderful journey that was to span over the years and still continues with the beautiful, lifelong friends that I have made.

What was to follow was beyond my wildest dreams. Being invited to the special events was truly awesome, the first being "An Audience with the Cast of A Place To Call Home" where I got to meet other members of the group for the first time, many of which have become dear friends that I will have in my life forever, meeting the cast and having photos taken etc. and being part of the filming of the show. This was the first of many.

I am very fortunate to live in Sydney and have been blessed with being able to attend the Foxtel Garden Party, the Foxtel BBQ, the Dinner Dance and Gala Fundraiser, all held at "Ash Park" aka Camelot. I also attended all of the Season Premiers, 3,4 & 5 held at Hayden Orpheum Theatre and Season 6 at The State Theatre, and a very intimate event for Sony's Season 6 DVD release at Tesutti Fabrics with Jenni Baird. My beautiful daughter, Kate accompanied me to all of these events and we have shared memories of special mother/daughter times together that we both will treasure. Through all of these amazing events I met more SAPTCHers, friendships grew and bonds were made that would go beyond APTCH events. These events would also take me out of my comfort zone and challenge me to become a bit more adventurous. I'm a jeans and T-shirts, no fuss, no dresses kind of girl and here I was dressing 50's style and wearing cocktail dresses and ball gowns and loving every minute of it.

Out of all these wonderful events I would have to say that my favourite would have to be a very intimate, non-official outing that was set to be just a bunch of SAPTCHers catching up for lunch, which turned out to be something amazing beyond belief with cast members turning up to surprise us, which was organised by Jeni Lewington and our beloved Noni. This was held at Nielsen Park, Vaucluse a location you may well recognise, and, along with Noni, we were joined by Deborah (Doris), Jenni (Regina), Sara (Caroline), Craig (Dr. Jack) and Aldo (Gino). It also became a non-official after party for Noni, who had just won a Logie for being inducted into the Logie's Hall of Fame. She even brought her Logie for us to see. This was very exciting and so overwhelming. We were so grateful to those cast members for giving up their precious time for us, but each time we thanked them, what they would say in return was how very grateful they were for our group to have saved the show and how it has helped to keep them in work for a few more years. This comment would be repeated by those, and other cast members, each and every time we would see them. They truly were filled with gratitude for our efforts in saving APTCH and it was so evident.

There are too many wonderful times that have come from being part of "The Save A Place To Call Home" group for me to write about them all, it would be a book in itself, and apart from all the official events and SAPTCH outings, of which there have been too many to count, thanks to our unofficial Events Planner, Brenda Fowler, there have also been the numerous other opportunities we've had to support cast members in their other ventures, such as "Mother" for Noni, numerous Cabarets, Plays and an Art Exhibition for Tim (Dr. Fox) a day time Song & Dance Show with Frankie J (Roy) and his lovely wife, Michelle, Plays for Marta (Sarah) and Ben (Rene), and Plays for Sara (Caro), just to name a few. Yet another example of how the success of the series has gone beyond APTCH, for the fans and cast alike.

The most amazing part of this journey is the people I've met, including some of the international fans, Donna, Jane and Susan from the USA, Angela and Graeme from the UK and Marjolein and Nell from the Netherlands (I missed out on meeting Gail from Israel), and the lifelong friends that I have made, friends that I would never have known if it wasn't for Peter Vernon creating "The Save A Place To Call Home" Facebook group. Thanks Peter from the bottom of my heart, I'm so glad to call you my dear friend.

In all this, and it's crazy to say it, but my gratitude also lies with Channel 7 for axing the show in the first place, for if it wasn't for their actions the SAPTCH group would have never come to be and we wouldn't have all gone on this incredible, wild ride. And of course, we're all forever grateful for Foxtel's foresight, and Brian Walsh's sister in particular for getting in his ear, and picking up the ball and running with it, they certainly scored numerous goals, with and for us all.

I know that as I read this book, and everyone else's stories, I'm going to be saying things like "Oh, I wish I'd said that!" "Oh yes, I remember that!" "Exactly how I feel!" "Absolutely!" etc., etc., etc. In other words what everyone else has contributed and the feelings and experiences they have had on this wonderful road trip, their stories will echo through me also. We have all been so tremendously touched by this APTCH/SAPTCH journey and the unexpected enormity of what has come of it. This much anticipated book is a clear example.

The SAPTCH group made history with its efforts in achieving something that has never been done before. That's the power of people, right there!!!

This beautiful period drama, "A Place To Call Home" has been a standout for Australian Television, and the fight, the save and the worldwide popularity is testimony to just how bloody damn good it is, and its complete story really does need to be preserved.

To Noni,

I'm so happy for the opportunity to express my greatest appreciation to you for making our SAPTCHer Luncheon so extra special. What a fabulous surprise it was to see you walk in the door and I'm so glad I captured the moment.

Our SAPTCHer get togethers are always so very special, even without cast members attending, but it was so nice of you, Deborah, Sara, Craig, Aldo and Jenni to give up your precious free time, time that could be spent relaxing in-between shoots or with family etc., to come and spend the day with us.

At the end of the day we joked about the Luncheon being your Logies After Party as you didn't get to attend one after your very well deserved and extremely overdue Induction into The Hall of Fame. I feel very privileged to have helped you celebrate at our informal "After Party" so to speak.

It was also a real treat to see your Logie up close and personal and we all had a lot of fun with it so thanks for bringing it along with you.

Noni, could you please pass on a very heartfelt "Thank You" to Deborah, Sara, Craig, Aldo and Jenni from Kate and me for giving up their time to come and spend the afternoon with us. They certainly kept the surprise element alive throughout the afternoon.

Hope you like the photos I've sent through.

Love and best Wishes,

Dolores :) xo

SUSAN SOUTHGATE

I was part of the small group who originally rallied outside Channel 7 with placards. It will be a day I'll never forget. This really got the ball rolling and very much annoyed Channel 7!! But we were very much seen by people all over Australia. It was great publicity as some were unaware the show had been cancelled and the reasons why.

From Little Things Big Things Grow

On October 26, 2014, people from the Queensland regional town of Maryborough participated in the culmination of the protest movement begun earlier that year to save the iconic Australian television series "A Place to Call Home", with a Protest Picnic held at a 1950's era café called Mary Delicious. Scheduled to take place at the same time in towns and cities across Australia, the picnics became a sweet celebration when news broke that Foxtel had stepped in to save the series. The focus of the picnic was not only to bring back a compelling home-grown drama, which happened to be the most-watched Australian drama series of 2013, but the protests had a wider message of supporting the local industry.

MARY BIRD AND GAY LYNCH

Mary Bird co-organised the picnic with Simone McArdle, a friend she made from the "Save A Place to Call Home" Facebook group established by Mr. Peter Vernon. Our picnic was wonderful and well supported and Mary and Simone were able to Skype with the show's stars Noni Hazlehurst and Ben Winspear on the day, a real thrill for those who attended. Mary was also instrumental in organising the Maryborough petition signed by hundreds of locals and visitors, all horrified at the premature axing of the show by the Seven Network and wanting to do their part to save the show. Mary arranged for three passionate protesters and followers of "A Place to Call Home" to have a photo taken to highlight the petition and it appeared on 8 October 2014 in the Maryborough Chronicle.

Friendships that begun all those years ago have remained as strong, be they close personal friendships or online friendships with people from all parts of the world. Many fantastic events to celebrate the success of "A Place to Call Home" have followed this first picnic and been enjoyed by thousands of fans. The fact that "A Place to Call Home" still retains a strong following across the globe is a testament to its excellence. People Power at work.

A Place to Call Home has a new address on pay TV

LAUREN COODLEY

I watched it alone when it first came out and loved it deeply. So when I entered chemotherapy for ovarian cancer, with my adult daughter as companion and caregiver, I invited her to watch it with me. We rationed the show so that we only watched half an episode in order to have the series end just after I had my last treatment. We wept together at the last episode, knowing we were crying not only for the characters, the nobility and beauty of the show, but for what we had just gone through together. Thanks to all the creators and actors who kept us company through this so difficult period, April to August 2020.

JESS WALES

Back in 2014 i decided to watch A Place To Call Home, purely for the fact that it was filmed in my local area. No real interest in the show or anything else for that matter. If it wasn't American, I wasn't interested. (Don't judge me ; I was 21 at the time and like most people, preferred US dramas).

But to my surprise, I was hooked from the first episode. I don't know if it was the music, the characters, the set, the storyline or the great actors, or a mixture?

But I wanted more.

I used to drive past multiple filming locations some days on my way to work, so wishing I could stop and watch.

Come end of Season 2, I loved the show and really wanted to meet the actors, and knew no one who watched the show for more than seeing familiar filming locations.

I remember sitting in a doctor's surgery or somewhere along those lines when I found out that the show wasn't going to be renewed.

I was shocked, angry, disappointed, sad and so many other emotions! I knew there was an important story that had to be told. The history of Australia through Bevan's eyes, with incredible twists and turns needed to reach more loungerooms!

It hadn't even had a chance to go international yet! I just knew we had something great and it wasn't the show's time to end.

I had never been so annoyed at a show ending before. I could see the potential it had for future seasons, and being a proud Aussie and local from Camden, I was passionate about doing what I could to give the show a chance.

So I started googling petitions and came across a few, one being Peter's I joined the Facebook page from there that Peter had mentioned in his email, at just a few hundred members.

Upon researching, i came across a few other Facebook pages and knew I wasn't the only one who needed to see the story continue.

I don't remember time frames as this all happened 6 years ago, and never in a million years did I think I'd have a story to tell today.

But not long after that, I knew I was in a unique position, living within 10 minutes of many filming locations. The show was putting our beautiful Camden town on the map, so I started thinking about how I could help!

I went to my local newspaper and told them about what was happening, and they loved my idea of getting exposure and people to sign the petition.

I had seen Jeni's posts about going to sunrise and protesting and decided that wasn' t for me. I would help in other ways.

I messaged Jeni about the newspaper article opportunity and wanting to get a few people together, (at this point I knew no one).

She mentioned she wasn't from Sydney but was coming down for the protest, and coincidentally also had lined up a photo opportunity with another local newspaper. Luckily, we were able to line them up the same day! Then Jeni convinced me to come to the Sunrise protest; I thought "Okay what do I have to lose? This could be a once in a life-time opportunity and might be fun!"

On 11th August 2014, I headed off to my local train station at 4am on a cold and rainy winter's morning thinking "What the hell am I doing? What 21-year-old does this?" and headed to the city. I was curious and excited to meet the founder of the page Peter Vernon, as well as fellow admins Jeni Lewington and Daniel Cooper, and other fans Sandy Hodkinson, Sue Southgate and Annette Van Lierop. I remember telling my family, as I 'd never done anything like this before, thinking they would think I'm crazy, or discourage me from meeting up with strangers, but they were fine with it.

I arrived with my green placard, to meet a bunch of strangers, to stand outside of Sunrise at 6am to protest and be broadcast across the nation. A morning of firsts!

For a while it didn't feel like we were having any impact and we were just being ignored. The channel 7 gods were not happy, as we were using their own platform against them.

I remember never having felt so cold in my life! But it was worth it! We piqued interest from spectators and got them on board with signs too! We felt powerful! Like we were making a difference. We received messages from others at home saying they could see us.

We caused a stir that morning!

It became bittersweet morning, because as we were finishing up, we received the breaking news of Robin Williams death.

I'll never forget that day.

A few days later, I met up with Jeni Lewington, Judy Grech, Catherine Matic and Sammy Nilsson with our youngest fan Victoria, outside of the gates of our beloved Camelot (Ash Park) for our photo shoots (another first). Meeting each other for the first time, getting photos together and answering questions for the journalists was super overwhelming but lots of fun! We felt like we made a difference! .

After the journalists had left, we noticed a gardener out the front. We started chatting to her about helping to save the show and soon realised it was the owner! Super lovely and happy for us to be helping! So that made our morning! The rest of us then head off to lunch to get to know one another better and reflect on what just happened! We then visited some filming locations and dropped off petitions.

Within a few weeks we were then planning our first Saptcher event, to gain exposure to save the show!

Picnics all over the country in each state!

Sammy and I took on Camden and became good friends as a result.

By now, we had a few thousand people writing, emailing, faxing, and calling channel 7, in addition to our protests, petitions, newspaper articles, word of mouth campaign Everyone doubted what could be done with people power, but we didn't let that stop us!

We were determined to see A Place To Call Home back on air for another season or four, where it belonged!

Days out from the picnic we found out we had saved show!

We actually did it!

Foxtel had picked up our beloved tv show thanks to the head of Foxtel Brian Walsh and his sister, who insisted he watch the show!

The picnic rolled around and we were a bit devastated to hear Sydney were getting cast members and we weren't, but still excited to have a fun day ahead as we got to Skype them instead!

It was a great day of new friendships, fun and celebration for all. Foxtel were ever so kind enough to supply us with cupcakes!

At the end of the picnic we had a surprise celebrity appearance from the man himself ,Brian Walsh!

Brian Walsh made the time to come to our celebratory picnic!

What! What an incredible honour!

So we stayed around chatting to him for a long time, such a down to earth and lovely guy.

Not long after, Sammy and I started hosting more location tours as we had the time and knew the area.

This was a lot of fun!

Every time we would go via the big beautiful gates of Camelot (Ash Park) and hope to one day get to see inside.

Then one day our lovely SAPTCHER friend/local/friend of the owners, Kylee Bentham surprised us at the gates and told us we were going in!

You can imagine how excited we all were!

That the beautiful owners were kind enough to open up their private property to us fans! An incredible day!

I have now been lucky enough to attend functions at least 5 times at the beautiful Camelot. So grateful.

The following year, September 2015 on Father's Day, we were lucky enough to attend a Garden Party organised by Foxtel at Camelot along with the actors, costumes, and cars from the set, had photos and autographs from the cast, and got to listen to David Berry sing Unchained Melody. A truly beautiful highlight!

Another highlight around the same time was being invited to Foxtel HQ to sit in the front row of the audience for an interview with the cast being filmed for Foxtel and was lucky enough to ask Abby Earl a question! I'd never been so nervous in my life but what an opportunity that was! Afterwards we got to hang around and chat to the cast and get photos. Talk about star struck!

Foxtel were so incredibly kind to us and organised so many incredible events for the fans. So many once in a lifetime opportunities that became part of our lives as we were so busy attending premieres, dinner dances, lunches, dinners, tours, filming locations, garden parties, awards nights, etc.

The first Dinner Dance we had at Camelot, meeting online friends from all over the country for the first time felt totally natural!

The second Camelot event we had was a Vintage Barbecue, when we had the fox himself Tim Draxl attend and grace us with his beautiful voice!

From there birthed the 'Foxy Girls' and his fan page, and he's been lucky enough to enjoy our presence at almost every one of his shows since (including his hometown Jindybyne) and has become a friend.

What's incredible is that in 2014 I was 21; I was struggling with a sense of identity. I wasn't entirely sure where I fit in the world, and when all of this came about, I quickly felt a sense of belonging, I was in my element and they were the best years of my life (so far).

To this day, I pinch myself that I got to have such incredible, once in a lifetime opportunities, and although we have the memories, it was hard not to take it all a tiny bit for granted at the time as it started to become the norm, and I miss it.

In saying that, I've met so many incredible lifelong friends along the way, on all parts of the journey, and am still making new ones to this day that feel like we have known each other forever.

Who knew the impact this show could have on a bunch of everyday people!

Thanks to a show I made lifelong friends and developed a sense of identity and of belonging along the way..

When the show ended people were worried that the events would stop and we would all go about our lives again.

Some broke off, but the rest of us...the only thing that stopped us was covid! We already have 2021 filled out with events.

I could probably talk forever about memories and opportunities I have been lucky enough to build on this 6 year journey...and I look forward to reading others stories, memories and highlights that I may have missed.

Thank you to every single person that has touched my heart along this journey, and look forward to many more, round the world even, when covid is over.

Forever my SAPTCHer family .

ANTONELLA DE LISEO

Where do I start with my incredible journey with A Place To Call Home?

Over the years I have been asked many times what I love about the show and I always reply, "How much time do you have?" There's just so much I love about it. First and foremost I loved the fact that it is Australian made as I love supporting all Australian productions and this is the best ever made. The writing is exemplary. Bevan Lee is a brilliant storyteller. The cast are the best in the business and absolute stars in their own right. I love the fact that we didn't need any international stars to promote this show because we have enough amazing talent right here from cast to crew which were all Aussies and all best in their field. The fashion was incredible and the wardrobe dept did a fabulous job in honoring that era. The 1950s was such an elegant and classical time. The show really captured the beautiful and timeless era from the gorgeous dresses to the splendid decor at Ash Park and not forgetting Caroline's amazing apartment. I was lucky enough to tour both locations and they just took my breath away. I adore this period.

I was hooked in the first ten minutes of Season 1 when it premiered in 2013. I was so excited about meeting these fabulous characters and finding out their story. Never did I imagine how much they all would come to mean to me. I couldn't wait to find out what this blonde bombshell Sarah Adams was going to do to this family and why they wanted her gone. Marta Dussledorp as Sarah was breathtaking and Noni Hazlehurst was the reason I tuned in to begin with - legend . Their storyline captivated my attention throughout the whole series. I just loved the good against the bad. I hadn't seen anything like this on Australian since The Sullivans, another great aussie show. I was also excited about the budding romance between Sarah and the handsome George Bligh played by Brett Climo. Sarah's green dress on the ship is my favorite to date. I was also intrigued with the storyline of the attempted suicide of James Bligh played by David Berry because of his struggles with his homosexuality and the deceit of keeping that a secret. This is something we really don't see much on TV and it was refreshing to see this topic tackled. I loved it and this is just Episode 1. I couldn't wait for the next episode and was the case for all six seasons. The show has tackled so many important issues that are still relevant today. Homophobia, domestic violence, discrimination, religious prejudices, aboriginal issues, and women's rights which are so important. I also loved Caro and Jack's love story. Their wedding was my favourite episode.

My journey really started when I heard that it was to be axed halfway through Season 2. I was devastated and shocked to realize that not everyone was enjoying it as much as I was. However I did accept it because at the end of the day it's just a TV show. Well how wrong I was! It's so much more than that. The story wasn't over.

I remember the sadness at watching the S2 finale. I was so outraged that they had ended this amazing show with such a boring and pathetic finale. None of it was true to character, it made no sense to the storyline and I felt that they had disrespected the fans of this show. It just left me wanting more. I woke the next morning still angry. No show has ever got me so worked up before. I started looking for a face book page about the show and was hoping they were doing something about it. To my delight I discovered the "Save a Place to Call Home" fb page where I voiced my opinion about the whole matter, and this is where I first met Peter Vernon who asked me to sign the petition he had started with Daniel Cooper. We were off. It was so wonderful to meet other fans on fb from all walks of life young and old who love the show as much as I do. I felt like I had met my own people in our own community. It was invigorating but never did I imagine how much they would come to meant to me. The lifelong friendships I have made are just special and incredible. I've met so many fans locally, nationally and I've got to converse with so many international fans which is just wonderful. It's really a unique relationship.

I wrote many letters to Channel 7, faxed, emailed and even did a mailbox drop off in my neighborhood asking everyone to please sign the petition to save the show. My friends and family were supportive, but a few did say that I was fighting a losing battle and wasting my time because it has never been done before. But we showed them. People Power at its best. I'll never forget waking up in Rome where I was holidaying at the time in 2014 to the news that Foxtel were picking up the show. I was crying and so happy and flabbergasted that we had actually done it. It had literally never been done before.

Unfortunately, I couldn't attend the picnics that had been organized statewide to protest the axing of the show as I was in Dubai returning home and it ended up becoming a celebration in saving the show. I was thrilled to see the cast had also joined in the celebrations which was so wonderful and amazing that they did that for the fans and to see them just as excited as we were. A brilliant moment in our story.

I've attended every event since that day. The first being the cast interview at Foxtel studios which aired just after the premiere of S3. It was such an emotional night--my first-time meeting fans face to face, in particular Peter Vernon and Daniel Cooper and Jeni Lewington our wonderful admins and of course seeing the cast in person for the first time. An amazing opportunity. You couldn't wipe the smile off my face all night. I got to meet Noni, Sara Wiseman, Craig Hall, David Berry, Abbey Earl, Aldo Mignone, Jenni Baird. It was a dream come true. Meeting Noni was just unbelievable. I had to pinch myself that I was standing there talking to her about all things APTCH. Just me and her. She was so gracious in her time and always has been. I remember asking her to bring her stage show Mother to Wollongong to which she did the following year.

Another incredible thing about the show was all the amazing events Foxtel put on and allowed fans to attend. It was unprecedented. There were premieres held in all states and I got to see it in my own local theatre in Wollongong. To my surprise Noni Hazlehurst was special guest. She actually remembered me from meeting her at Cast interview. I was gob smacked that she remembered me but that is Noni for you. The premier of Season 3 was such an emotional night for me. I cried when it started because I didn't think we'd ever get a Season 3. The realization that it was happening because we helped save the show makes me teary even now. Nobody understands that feeling. Only SAPTCH fans get it (our nickname for ourselves became SAPTCHERS). Episode 1 of Season 3 certainly did not disappoint either. It was fantastic. It was also where I met Jess Wales who is one of my besties now. Also meeting other SAPTCHERS i.e. Kerrie Hartin, Teena Luck, Sonia Krawenchko, Anne Perry, Cindy Blaney.

As I said there are so many events, I've had the privilege of attending but I will briefly mention the highlights.

The Garden Party at Camelot aka Ash Park before S3 premiered - actually walking around the grounds of 'Ash Park' and standing in front of the house was a dream come true. Meeting the cast again and Lucky the dog too was so special, David Berry singing Unchained Melody was sublime and of course meeting more fans and this is where I met Brenda Fowler first time who has become one of my dearest friends.

Touring the Mahratta House where Carolines Apartment was filmed. The decor is AMAZING!,

The Season 4 barbeque at Camelot where I got to actually go inside Ash Park this time and walk around the dining room, the bedrooms and the kitchen was so special. The cast attended AGAIN along with Bevan Lee and Tim Draxl. First time I met Tim and got to hear him sing. He is an incredible performer.

Neilsen's Cafe lunch was another day which was only meant to be a SAPTCHER catch up but the cast surprised us and attended as well. I mean have you ever heard a cast doing that before for their fans. Just showing up in their Sunday casual clothing to join us just like they would with their friends . Jenni Baird even brought her kids along. It was just so amazing. I was gobsmacked to see Noni walk in and say hello to me (she remembered me again) followed by Deborah Kennedy aka Doris, Sara Wiseman (Caroline), Craig Hall (Dr Jack Duncan), Aldo Mignone (he is so cheeky), and Jenni Baird. They were all so lovely and happy to talk about their characters and the show. It was just so amazing that they gave up their precious time off set to meet us, Noni even brought her Gold Logie and I got to hold it. I recall a very special moment for myself with Noni when she noticed a photo of my kids on my phone and her asking me about the kids. So sweet of her to take an interest in my life. So here we are talking about motherhood just like I would with my own friends. I just had to pinch myself. Noni is just so down to earth and always makes you feel important. She gives the best hugs too. I could go on and on about how much I adore her she is just brilliant actress, woman and human. A great role model.

The first Cocktail Party held at Camelot where Noni, Sara and Craig attended was a gala event. Such a glorious night all of us dressed in our finest outfits. I loved my red 50s dress which I wore in honor of Regina's fabulous red dress in S4. I even got to dance with Noni. The after party was so much fun too. A fabulous night from start to finish.

The second cocktail party held in 2018 again at Camelot was also an amazing night. Jack Ellis, AKA "Stan O'Rourke" was the special guest of honor. He looked so handsome and he is a wonderful painter too. (I'm the proud owner of two) That night was so special as they had a lot of memorabilia on auction and I won a few things. For example, The drawings of Olivia and James, the plaque of Dawn Briggs Community College and signed manuscript by all the cast of Season 6. So fortunate to have these pieces in my home.

I think I would have to say my favorite event was attending the TV Week Logie Awards in the Gold Coast. I have always dreamt of being there and because of this show I was able to do so thanks to Vanessa Hollins at Foxtel and Jeni Lewington for making it happen. It was truly amazing to be there and see the cast all dressed up in their glamour and getting to talk to them especially Marta Dusseldorp who has always eluded me. She was beaming with excitement and when I asked her about Season 6, I told her I wasn't looking forward to the finale and end of our show and she simply said "You will love it. Its wonderful". And she was right ; I did love it.

The Season 6 premiere at The State Theatre was just like a Hollywood red carpet event. So glamorous and star studded. We were all dressed in our best 50s wear and most of the cast were there. A very special night. Foxtel had organised a bus to transport us there and back from Wollongong which was an unbelievable thing to do for us.

The road trip to Jindabyne to see Tim Draxl perform his cabaret performance is another special memory with my fellow SAPTCHer buddies Brenda Fowler, Jess Wales and Nicole Smith. I never thought I'd ever do anything like that. He is an amazing performer! We had decided to dress in a black and white Hollywood theme and we were definitely best dressed that night! The next day Tim invited us to lunch with his dear mum Del and I invited him to our first Tim Draxl "Foxy" Fan Club luncheon I was organizing (which I've done the past 4 years).I wasn't expecting him to make it, but he surprised us and attended in Wollongong. Just one more example of the cast going above and beyond for their fans. That road trip was the start of an amazing friendship for the four of us girls. I know we will be lifelong friends. We talk every day!

I have been so lucky to experience all these events and I am so glad I pushed myself to do so. The show has had a profound effect on my life. It's boosted my self -confidence and made me try things I would never have dreamt of. I just can't imagine my life without this show and the amazing friendships that I've made throughout. It really isn't "just a tv show" It's a community of people who have come together because of the love of this show. The friendships and bonds that have been formed are the best thing about this show. I've formed so many amazing friendships! One person in particular is Dolores Ryan, who is just the most wonderful friend. We met through the show and became besties after a very unpleasant experience with a despicable overseas guest who was here because of the show. I will always treasure her friendship.

What's so great about this community of fans is how we've been able to keep the SAPTCH page going even after the show finished. and I love the APTCH COMMUNITY PAGE which was created for international fans. I was so worried that we would all lose touch and the page would but it's just gotten even stronger. We all still catch up for birthdays and lunches. We try to support the cast in their own theatrical productions although this year we weren't able to due to Covid. Speaking of Covid, it's amazing that it somehow brought us even closer together! Jess Wales initiated Zoom Chats which have allowed us to talk not only with Aussie fans but people from all over the world. . I have really loved that. We've even had virtual chats with Bevan Lee, Noni Hazlehurst, Tim Draxl and Frankie J Holden .) big thank you to Kerrie Hartin, Peter Vernon and Jess Wales for organizing it so well. I don't know of any other show where the fans have so much interaction with the cast at no cost at all. It just blows my mind every time!

I will always treasure all the memories and truly feel so blessed to have had this wonderful experience. No other show comes close.

MARGARET PENNISON

I think it was in the early spring of 2017 during a regular weekly phone chat with my sons mother-in-law that she asked if I was following an Australian TV drama called A Place To Call Home which was really good. I am normally a radio listener during the daytime unless tennis or cricket are showing, but I decided to try this highly recommended drama. My memory isn't what it was, but I think it was season 3 on at the time. It must have been special because I just couldn't wait for the next episode 7 days later, and my granddaughter ordered seasons 1 and 2 for me from Amazon, I think. I was hooked. I googled and went on YouTube looking for what I could find relating to the show. I then did something that shocked my family. I asked one of them to enroll me on Facebook so that I could join the APTCH fan club. I used to grumble at them when they visited me because they spent so much time on that "blumming Facebook" as I called it. I think that was 2018. She announced on her page "I can't believe it. Nan has joined Facebook." It may seem a trivial thing to do for many, but I really do struggle with technology, and my family often have to come to my rescue.

This drama APTCH, the authors lead by Bevan Lee, the amazing actors, the fan club, everyone involved in this, for me, best ever period drama, watched in 140 countries all over the world, has given me a new interest which I love, and you could say I'm addicted. Never before have I viewed a programme repeatedly as I have this one. I have it all downloaded, and I also purchased 2 box sets, in case one wears out. There is something truly special about the way Bevan Lee puts over the story of the lives of his characters in the way he does. I cried a lot, and I also laughed a lot. 67 episodes, yet I still wanted more. Just didn't want it to end.

I wouldn't be writing thus if it hadn't been for an absolutely amazing group of many devoted fans who were determined to keep this drama going when it originally concluded at the end of season 2. They apparently put so much pressure on the powers that be, that it was taken over and continued for another 4 seasons, making it 6 seasons in all 2013-2018.

Thank you so much, every single one of those amazing, devoted fans. We all owe you so much. PS: as a music lover, I just couldn't close without thanking Michael Yezerski for the beautiful music, over 30 pieces that he composed especially for APTCH. I have them all on my favourite playlist.

BRIDGET McNAMARA
My Journey to A Place To Call Home

Having lived in Europe for some years, I was late to the party with A Place To Call Home and missed the original airing of Season 1.

Back home in Sydney, Australia, in 2014, I was watching Downton Abbey, which was airing on a Free-To-Air commercial channel here, and when the Season finished, promos for Season 2 of A Place To Call Home were shown. The costumes and lighting impressed me so I messaged my daughter and asked her what it was like. Her response was 'Oh, you'll probably like that, it's your era'! I might add that I was a *very* young child during the 1950s and my daughter was having a dig at me, as we Aussies say.

Nevertheless, I started watching from about Season 2, Episode 2 I think, really enjoyed it, went out and bought the Season 1 DVDs and was thoroughly hooked.

I was happily watching Season 2 Episode 10 in July when I realized this must be the final episode of the season – some shows do 12 episodes per season, even 13, I never know what to expect – but, thinking that there would be the promised Season 3, I was content to just sit back and watch.

Things started to go horribly wrong, however, in the last six minutes of the episode: it was like watching a Charlie Chaplin movie, speeded up. Nothing made sense, characters and story arcs were suddenly going off on inexplicable tangents, and it seemed as if a bewildering array of 'closures' was being offered. I felt a little breathless trying to keep up and then suddenly, the 'curtain' fell, the credits ran and, most unforgettably, the words 'T h e E n d' scrolled across the screen in an ever-so-slightly melodramatic manner and a Gone With The Wind-type font! I clearly remember sitting there staring at the screen thinking, 'what the…?!'

I've been 'disappointed' with the endings of a couple of other television shows (OK, if you insist: Lost and True Blood - yes, I have eclectic tastes) but I was *outraged* at this ending, coming, as it did for me, out of the blue. I'm not a huge television fan and so hadn't seen the announcements in various media that the plug had been pulled on the show half-way through the season and that the ending had had to be hastily re-written and re-filmed to accommodate the cancellation and tie up any loose storylines. (It didn't work, by the way.)

So I immediately got online and googled 'why has A Place To Call Home ended?' I found the various reports and also a link to a fan petition to 'save' the show. In an entirely uncharacteristic move – because I usually don't care *that* much - I signed the petition. That had a link to a private Facebook group dedicated to saving the show and in an even less characteristic move, I joined that as well.

I found myself among about another 300 or so people who felt as passionate as I did about the show's abrupt cancellation, which I found interesting. Not surprisingly, almost all were women, of my generation, and with similar interests in the Arts. However, most surprisingly, the petition and Facebook group had been created by a 45-year-old Dad – one Peter Vernon, variously known as Our Fearless Leader, PeteVee, The Cult Leader (coined by my daughter)* and Superman. Peter lives in Newcastle a couple of hours' drive North of Sydney. Jeni Lewington, of Brisbane, Dan Cooper, of Sydney, and Imogen Crest, of rural Victoria, joined Peter as Admins of the Facebook group. The four of them have been keeping us in line, more or less, ever since, and the group now boasts 7,500 members, from all corners of the globe.

*For reasons which are not obvious at this point in my story, my adult children started referring to our group as a 'Cult' – but not of the dangerous, brain-washing variety – and when Peter called me one day when I was in the car with my daughter, she said, 'Oh, it's the Cult Leader is it.' (She shares Peter's birthday, so I am forever cursed with not being able to forget Peter's!) This became a long-running joke between Pete and me, one which we shared with the group from time to time:

Peter asked Bridget to devote a shrine to him...

Our work to save the show quickly gained momentum as we pulled together to inundate the network with complaints about the show's cancellation, and to ask for its resurrection. Phone calls were made, faxes were sent, and snail-mail letters written.

We arranged 'mail-in' days, when everyone would post a letter to a specific person/people at the network on the same day. Given Australia's size and the fact that we had members in Alice Springs in the 'Red Centre' of the country 2,772 km (1,722 miles) from Sydney where the show was filmed, and in Far North Queensland, 2,414 km from Sydney, and in Perth, Western Australia, 3,933 km from Sydney, we knew that they wouldn't all arrive on the same day but they were all dated the same, which we believed was a show of the strength of the organised opposition to the show's cancellation.

Members of the Facebook group quickly formed friendships with other like-minded people across the country and shared stories of the 1950s, recipes, and family photos. A fondness for the fashions of the era was discovered, while others discovered they had musical and literary tastes in common.

By October of that year, the group had grown significantly and the 'protest' over the show's cancellation was in full swing. We all received the standard response form from the Network, which didn't tell us anything we didn't already know it boiled down to the demographic the show was allegedly attracting not being attractive enough for advertisers. This reasoning enraged those of us 'of a certain age' even more! Furthermore, it made no sense: why does a network buy a show depicting a certain era and *not* expect that a large percentage of viewers of that show might also *be* of that era? And in any case, we had teenagers in the group.

So we decided to organise an Australia-wide Protest Picnic for the 26th of October. Some international members were going to join in in their own way. We decided that this Picnic should, of course, be 50s-themed, and we excitedly discussed, on the Facebook page, what we would wear, what food we would bring, locations, decorations, banners, T-shirts and so on. Pens were made, flyers were distributed, radio stations were contacted, we held a 'Twitter-thon' to advertise the Picnics, and excitement was high in a number of locations around this vast country. Weather forecasts for the day, for all areas, were regularly posted on the page and people who were unable to attend were organising to Skype with those in attendance or to submit a photo of themselves, taken on the day, raising a glass to APTCH.

Then, in the final frenetic days of organising the picnics, on 15 October 2014, it was announced that Foxtel had bought the rights to A Place To Call Home and had undertaken to produce at least a further two seasons! No-one who hadn't written hundreds of letters nor spent the previous month deciding what bag and shoes to wear to the picnic, could possibly understand what that announcement meant to us: we were, firstly I think, gobsmacked – we'd done it, we'd 'saved' the show! We had, unknowingly, made Australian television history. And there were tears – lots and *lots* of tears! Posts and messages flew thick and fast over the next 24 hours and the 'Protest Picnics' became 'Celebration Picnics': the 'Save' on t-shirts which had read 'Save A Place To Call Home' quickly had a 'd' added at the end, and we started calling ourselves 'SAPTCHers' – which doesn't exactly roll off the tongue, but it is how even the cast refer to us now.

The day, naturally, dawned bright and clear – and, being Spring in Australia, for most of us anyway, hot. So it was a sparkling day of truly joyous celebration of the triumph of 'the people'. The mood across the country was euphoric – this might all sound a little over the top for a television show, but it was an important victory: many of us did, and still do feel, that the age group of the demographic the show was attracting was an issue for the commercial network: our local networks skew their programming heavily towards the under 45 year-old age bracket, with most of it being dominated by 'reality shows', so we felt the decision to cancel the show was ageist. It also showed an alarming lack of support for television drama generally and for Australian drama in particular.

We also felt for the very talented team who'd put the show together: from the writer, Bevan Lee, to the actors, and the vast number of highly talented artists who recreated the look of the 1950s with such precision and beauty, it was a large and expensive undertaking which we felt had not been allowed to truly blossom. It seemed ludicrous for all that hard work to have gone to waste. So knowing that we had assured another 2 seasons' work for the artists and 2 seasons' watching pleasure for ourselves, was a very rewarding feeling.

The real 'icing on the cake' was that unbeknownst to us, various cast members had been coopted to attend the picnics in our two major cities, Sydney and Melbourne, and Foxtel had also organised specially decorated cupcakes to be delivered to those centres and to the picnic held at Camden, on Sydney's Western outskirts, where the house and property used as 'Ash Park' are located. You can imagine the thrill when the artists arrived!

After the picnic, the page was flooded with hundreds of photos from picnics around the country – and from at sea, from Germany, from Korea, from backyards, from loungerooms – and that's when my role within the group started to become more specialised. There were so many happy smiling faces I decided to 'memorialise' the day by collecting a sample of the photos and putting them together into a video montage set to a 1950s soundtrack. Thus the first of many video montages and other musical contributions was born.

I am happy to say that I have similarly memorialized many of our most significant 'occasions' and they have become, if I may be permitted to say so, a popular feature of the page.

Around a year later, in late 2015, Season 3 was ready to premiere and Foxtel held a promotional Garden Party at Camelot, the house and property that serve as Ash Park in the show. Other groups and individuals were invited – the local Historical Society, the local Country Women's Association Branch members, people who'd entered and won Foxtel competitions – but, naturally, the SAPTCHers felt it was all about us! We had members come from Perth, Adelaide, rural Victoria, Melbourne, Sydney, rural NSW, Newcastle, Byron Bay, Wollongong, Brisbane, rural Queensland and many places in between (we Sydneysiders also had to book hotel rooms out there, as did the inter-state visitors, because Camden is quite a long way from the City) and the hysteria mounted! This time we knew the cast would be in attendance, Foxtel was providing morning tea, we were free to roam the grounds, plus, for most of us, it was the very first time that we had met each other in the flesh. Some of us were also privileged enough to share a special VIP lunch and tour of the house with the cast afterwards.

I ended up setting up several 'Event' pages on Facebook so that we could organise transport and accommodation for those who needed it, and also to discuss that most important of topics – what to wear! The occasion was, of course, 50s-themed. Sadly, it wasn't a SAPTCHer who won Best Costume either!

Meeting some of my virtual BFFs was one of the highlights of the weekend, as it was for everyone. Most of us arrived the day before as the Garden Party was due to start quite early in the morning, so about 40 of us had dinner together the night before. I remember that Pam Schultz, who had come from Adelaide and with whom I had formed a firm friendship in the early days, had saved me a seat next to her at the pub where we had dinner – except that it was like catching up with an old friend, not meeting someone new. Similarly, another bestie, Jenni Goodwin, also an out-of-towner, drove me to Camelot on the morning of the Garden Party and it was as if we'd known each other for years. When Imogen Crest and I finally managed to find each other, we both screamed! Plus most of the rooms at the motel I stayed at were filled with SAPTCHers so there was much hooting and laughter throughout the afternoon before as we all arrived – and there may have been alcohol and nibblies involved as well!

Some of us had actually met the previous week at the Fox studios where an 'Audience With the Cast' was filmed: a few of us presented questions to the cast which had been submitted by SAPTCHers from all over the country – we even had 2 inter-staters at that – and that aired the week before Season 3 premiered on Fox. We screamed ourselves hoarse at that too but that's because they kept having to do take after take after take of the cast members being introduced, and enthusiastically greeted, and every time something would go wrong! Who'd work in television?!

The Garden Party weekend was, I think, the best time we've ever had– because it was 'The First'. The first time we'd come together, from all over the country, as SAPTCHers; the first time most of us had met; the first time we'd gotten together to celebrate A Place to Call Home; the first time we'd really celebrated our 'victory'.

So, naturally, it required a video montage – a very long video montage, at around 30 minutes, but no-one seemed to mind. And it certainly demonstrated what an absolutely fabulous weekend we'd all had.

Other montages followed over the years and we still break them out from time to time: everyone sheds a few tears and we go about our business. I have also taken on the role of honorary music contributor and try to find clips to share that I know SAPTCHERs will love, especially on significant occasions or when times are tough.

There is a rather large core group based here in Sydney, and others in Melbourne, rural communities, Adelaide among other places, which meets regularly (pre-COVID and via Zoom since COVID) to kick up their heels and celebrate the amazing and life-long friendships that have been born out of this rather odd situation: people banding together to protest the cancelling of a television show.

"From little things, big things grow" in the words of Australian songwriter, Paul Kelly. [1]

---

[1]   "From Little Things Big Things Grow" written by Paul Kelly & Kev Carmody, Mushroom, 1991.

KYLIE BENTHAM

Kylie Bentham:

The part of my story that's special is being from the town where most of the show was filmed.

I was watching what, unbeknownst to me , would be the last episode of A place to Call Home. At the end of the show, it was announced that this was the last episode of the series.

We all looked at each other in complete shock. At that point I messaged the Powers family to find out what was going on. Their response was that, yes, it had been axed and they were also very sad. I thought, NO, this can't be happening! what can we do to help. As I was looking on Facebook, I saw a post come up from another group already starting the fight to bring back a place to call home and I joined immediately. "Well, the rest is history" The power of the group together doing submissions and growing to over 7.5K soon made people listen.

To think such a great show was gone! Everyone was in disbelief. The show not only gave me something my girls and I could enjoy together but living in the town Camden for over 16 years knowing the place and the family who lived where the show was being filmed meant the show was very close to my heart. I wanted to help find out why it was axed and hopefully help bring it back.

Some lovely memories were the amazing people and cast I met along the way and making them all smile when The Powers Family gave me the opportunity to bring some of the group into Camelot house (AKA Ash Park) for a little tour of the grounds and their lovely home.

Another one was being able to help with the Foxtel event at the garden party, co-ordinating the cast and looking after all the excited fans from the group.

Special thanks from me also to the group and the Powers family or providing their home so we could have fundraisers to help the Shining Stars Foundation, a charity that I co-founded that gives back to the homeless and less fortunate.

SONIA KRAWCZENKO

It seems forever ago that our battle to save A Place to Call Home started. I remember being halfway through the 2nd season when a friend of mine, who lives in Camden and often saw them filming, informed me that the show had been axed and there wouldn't be a 3rd. OMG my heart sank in that moment. I was in sheer disbelief. How could they even THINK about cancelling such an awesome Australian, show? The keyboard warrior in me got straight onto Facebook and searched to see if there were any groups that could disprove this atrocious rumour. What I found was the "Save A Place to Call Home Group". It must be true then if a group had been started......wahhhhhhh. I joined the group and was introduced to Peter and Jeni and caught up with the goings on so far. They had just done a protest at the Channel 7 studio with placards and everything....awesome. They were now calling on everyone in the group to write letters to Channel 7 asking them not to cancel the show and telling them what stupid bloody idiots they are (well, ok, I may have exaggerated that bit but let's face it , they were!!). I don't know how many letters I wrote...... A LOT ! That was life for awhile. Then came the picnics. To be carried out nationwide on the same day with one mission in common....to bring awareness that this amazing show was being cancelled and the people did not like it....not one bit! We were all so excited. We were all counting down. Planning our outfits, how would we get there, would any media come? Then......a rumour started. I think The sister of Brian Walsh, head honcho at Foxtel, that had heard of our campaign and watched the series. She loved it (of course) and told her dad he HAD to watch it and try and save it. The rest, as they say, is history. Brian watched it, loved it and set in motion talks with Channel 7 for a possible collaboration. First time in history that paid tv had made such an agreement with a free to air channel. OH MY GOODNESS.......those picnics then ended up being a WE SAVED A PLACE TO CALL HOME celebrations. I attended the Camden picnic and met some of the amazing people of the group. Brian Walsh came too and we got sent some amazing Place to Call Home cupcakes given to us by Foxtel. We also had a FaceTime chat with the Sydney group who were lucky enough to have some of the cast members show up. AH - MAZING. The rest was such a whirlwind. Over the months we had premier showings of each new season's first episode. The most amazing one being the first episode of season 3 where we got to watch the alternate ending to season 2. GOOSE PIMPLES!! WE DID THIS. WE MADE THIS HAPPEN. OH.MY.GOD!! We had 2 Gala dinners. The first one was absolutely amazing as most of the cast turned up, David Berry sang, we drank, we laughed. We hobnobbed with the cast. The second one included an auction of props and I won the Bligh Family Bible. It's a massive old Bible and has family pictures and the family tree. It's on display in my living room.

Tim Draxl has personally come to local events we have done here in Wollongong....I mean, how lucky are we? Members have continued to support the actors by attending various shows and concerts they have done but they appreciate us as much as we do them Sara and Craig continue to post messages to us all wishing us Merry Christmas etc. etc. Noni has always given us so much of her time, as have all the cast. It has been an amazing ride. I was so sad when the final season ended BUT it ended so perfectly. It ended the way it should have been ended. It did the show, Bevan Lee, and the actors justice. Oh, and did I mention.........IT WON A GOLD LOGIE (as it deserved).

I will forever feel extremely proud that I was a part of saving this amazing show.

LUCY DILLON

RACHEAL DWYER

First Picture: The Gala with SAPTCH administrators Daniel Cooper and Peter Vernon

Second: Celebrating After Tim Draxl's Concert with 2 visitors from Holland

The Definition of Happiness for SAPTCHers

JUDY GARTAGANIS
'A Place to Call Home'

My involvement began when I heard that production of the series was to end with the last episode of Season 2.

I wondered why the series was axed and what other viewers thought of the last episode.

In my search, I soon found a Facebook group with members expressing similar views and outrage.

Letters were sent to the station voicing our disappointment and requesting its return. It was suggested that with continuous letter writing, we will be heard…. and so the letters poured in daily with little or no reply from the Station.

Members from the newly formed FB group planned to meet at the Television Station where the Series was produced.

As I recall, it was 6am on a wet, cold winter's morning - they stood outside the Morning Show set that was airing with the intention of being seen by viewers and possibly Management.

Standing outside, under their wind-blown umbrellas in pouring rain, behind the huge glass windows and holding onto their coloured signed boards - they were seen in the background of the studio set smiling and waving to viewers.

It was satisfying to know that they received some external coverage and we certainly felt their determination and effort in such difficult conditions.

The next day - the ghastly wet and cold conditions had surprisingly cleared and the sun shone bright. Plans were made for members to meet up at Camelot in Camden where filming took place for 'Ash Park'.

As it was about 40 minutes away from my home - I thought it was a good idea to meet up and show my support, even though I had only just decided that morning.

We met at 11am and it turned out to be a day full of surprise and achievement, both personally and for the Group.

As expected, the property was closed to the public but we were happy to see the Home from the locked cast iron gates ahead of the Driveway.

During our time there, we met with 2 local newspaper reporters, one before and one after lunch. Both were keen to report the reason behind our campaign to the Local Community as they had provided most of the services and accommodation to the cast and crew whilst in Production.

Later that afternoon, whilst we were still at the front gate and planning to leave – we met with the Lady Owner of the Property as she was tending her garden. We explained why we were there and she supported our views regarding the quality, content and continuation of the series.

Although we were only a small group of 6 – we felt that we scored a goal just by being there.

It was satisfying to connect with members who had never met prior to that day - simply due to the common thread and praise of the show.

The following week our Group Interview and Photos were printed on the Front Page of both newspapers. (See attachments)

This led to more interest from members to arrange themed events and a Nationwide Wide Picnic Day in October to promote more exposure of the Series.

Fortunately, one of our members mentioned our Group to her Brother, who she thought might be able to help. He followed her suggestion and bought the DVD's soon after. I understand that he was pleasantly surprised and also became keen to see the series continue.

He met with the appropriate connections and providing all the exact cast and crew were on board to continue, it was announced that Production would resume.

As it turned out, her Brother happened to be an Executive at Foxtel Television.

So by the time the Nationwide Picnic was due in October - it suddenly became a picnic Celebrating the Series being saved by "Foxtel".

Our picnic was held in MacArthur Park, Camden and it turned out to be a super special one.

Upon arrival, we soon received a huge delivery of crème filled cupcakes adorned with the Foxtel Logo and later on had a surprise visit from the Man that made it all happen.

He discussed his excitement of the show, took a group photo with us and left us feeling over the Moon with elation from the Day's events.

We later met with the owners of the property and they generously shared stories of the history and restoration of their beautiful home and property.

The following year, series 3 was filmed on schedule and the show continued for another 3 seasons.

Foxtel kindly presented us with advanced cinema screenings prior to televising each series on their Station. This included screenings in most capital cities, Australia wide.

We also met with attending Cast members and had Q & A sessions and Photo signings.

They enjoyed our involvement and support of the series as much as we did.

Thanks to our Admin team for their encouragement and to Foxtel for completing the series and supporting Australian Drama - we would not have this unprecedented experience had the show not been 'Axed'.

I am honoured and privileged to have met so many beautiful people and to be a member of such a pleasant group.

KARYN PAGANO

My relationship with A Place To Call Home started from the very first episode back in April 2013 when I fell in love with the story being told. I used to watch the show religiously, as did my mother, who always told me her favourite was 'the doctor' being Craig Hall. In April 2014 my mother passed away and when the show returned in May 2014, I was extremely sad that I could no longer talk to her about her favourite character. The second season finished in July 2014 and we were all told the show would not return, much to the upset and outrage of its Australian fans, as we could see the storyline still had a long way to go.

A short time later, I came across a petition to sign to help renew the show for more seasons. This had never been done before in Australia. I joined the Facebook group, The Save A Place To Call Home group, started by Peter Vernon, and from there we fought and fought for the show to come back on our screens. Little did I know then that this fight would take me on a wonderful journey of meeting new people, attending wonderful events, making and keeping newfound friends and finding a way to have something to do whilst grieving for my mum.

I bought a card, which was the image of where Elizabeth, played by the wonderful Noni Hazelhurst, would sit and drink her tea and wrote my own personal little plea to help save the show. It was such a surprise to receive a personalised thank you card from Brian Walsh at Foxtel, who was the person we can all thank for taking up the renewal of the show.

The first event I attended, was at Observatory Hill in Sydney in October 2014, after Foxtel had announced they were taking over production of the show. There were picnics held all over Australia as a way to celebrate this wonderful occasion. Many of the cast members came to our event and others went where there could. This day was the start of me attending many social gatherings and formal events where we would often be in the company of one or some of the cast members. Their appreciation of what we had done for the show, was returned to us by their many attendances to our events, some big and small. My husband who never watched the show, has also enjoyed many of the events we have attended including a four -day cruise with a group of us SAPTCHers.

I am very lucky to have purchased at the auctions at our two Gala events at Camelot (Ash Park), one of only two paintings of Roy Briggs played by Frankie J Holden, the typewriter used by Anna played by Abby Earl, the cigarette holder, lighter and case used by Regina played by Jenni Baird.

As recently as yesterday, I attended a lunch with some of my friends and then we attended the art exhibition of Tim Draxl who played Dr Henry Fox.

It is a very proud thing to have been part of such a milestone in Australian television, which forged the way to our show being able to continue its story as it should and it being screened all over the world and achieving the following it has.

It has been and still is a privilege to be part of such a wonderful group from the very beginning.

RUBY YAP

MARILYN MORGAN

In mid-2014 I was stunned to think a series I was enjoying so much was going to be scrapped. Well, not on my watch it wasn't. I had seen a few people chatting online re the chopping of the 1950's drama. We took up arms and with the help of dedicated fans we did all we could to reinstate it and achieved the ultimate : saving of the show. So with letters, protests and a planned picnic that encompassed the whole of Australia we set out to do what was unprecedented and save A Place To Call Home. I believe our picnic on the Gold Coast had the tiniest gathering, but we counted in the scheme of things. By this time the word was out that we achieved our goal, and the series was to continue.

From those hectic and sometimes frantic beginnings we grew to an amazing group of fans who immersed ourselves into the theme of the drama. Many dressing in the style of the era. We partied, picnicked, went to premiers and met and mingled with the famous and ultimately joining our Stars on the red carpet at the AACTA Awards and the Logies. Our greatest thrill was to be invited to A Garden Party at the venue 'Ash Park' Camelot at Camden.

I have formed lifetime friendships and bonds with so many of the fans. I have organised events like Vivid in Sydney and joined many High Tea Parties.

What a huge honour it has been to be part of Television History and be instrumental in Saving A Place To Call Home.

There are so many stories to tell, places we've been and seen and Stars we have met. It was a wonderful journey and one to be proud of and remember with pride.

Holding the Banner high at our
Melbourne Xmas party.

With Frankie J Holden

CASSANDRA GRAHAM

I would like to write about the wonderful friendships i have made from a Facebook group for our beloved show "A Place To Call Home"

I joined this Facebook group during season 3. However, I had watched the series on TV from the beginning when it was aired on Channel 7 for the first 2 seasons, then got axed and Foxtel picked it up due to the high public demand saving it from people who i now lovingly call my friends. Shortly after that I went to an afternoon tea at the hall at Cobbitty near Camden where the show is mainly filmed. It was a CWA style afternoon tea and many of the people wore their 50's style dresses and outfits to look like they stepped out of that era. I was welcomed by many but mainly Brenda Fowler, Nicole Smith, Jess Wales, Dolores Ryan and Anne Seacome who were all responsible for putting on such a wonderful afternoon. I immediately felt at home in their company and enjoyed a splendid afternoon tea and a chat with lots of people. Then had a tour of the Blighs church right next door.

Since that wonderful afternoon i have enjoyed so many memorable occasions with my new friends such as seeing one of the stars of the show Tim Draxl in 2 of his plays Lip Service & Evie May. Christmas Luncheons on riverboats, movie trips, Titanic Exhibition, the show premiers for the last 3 seasons, seeing Noni Hazelhurst's play "Mother" and the wonderful Gala Charity Dinner.

My husband and I also joined in 2 of the Garden Parties that were held at Camelot the beautiful home and gardens of Ash Park, they were lots of fun with dress ups, prizes, entertainment, food and the stars making themselves freely available to mingle, entertain, sign autographs and take photos with. Without a doubt another high light of our show.

I have a very dear friend now Angela who out of the blue sent me a friend request through Facebook from Cornwall England, I don't normally accept friend requests from people I don't know or never met, but I did. She has become someone close, and we struck up a very quick friendship on Facebook and writing to each other in private that when she said she was arranging to come to Sydney to the come to the gala, I was quick to offer that she and her husband Graeme come and stay at my place for a few days, and I would take her out and about. We had a lovely 3 days together doing things and just getting to know each other better At one stage in the weekend I asked, what she would like to watch on the tv whilst I did a few things. Sure enough she said an episode of "A Place to Call Home" which was currently on at the time, and they hadn't got that series in England yet. (lucky I had taped it). Went to the Gala the following week and had a fantastic time and the next day we caught up again with most of the group and had lunch. Angela was lucky enough to join a group who were doing a tour of the Camden area and seeing some of the sights that the show is filmed in and that are depicted in another friend from our group Jeni Lewington's book 'APTCH Location Guidebook."

In 2019, there were 24 of us that went on a cruise to Moreton Island QLD, and we enjoyed each other's company with some partners for 4 wonderful days of eating, drinking, partying, swimming and relaxing and I have to say it was the best cruise I had been on. We hope to do it again as a group one day.

I have so many beautiful friends on Facebook from our group, they are the most wonderful caring friends, all looking out for each and ready to offer help or words of support and kindness, which is something I treasure immensely. I have so many wonderful memories and memorabilia from the show and all of these occasions and lots of photos to treasure. I'm sure this will continue for many years to come which I'm forever grateful.

Karyn Pagano, Lesly Kerl, Sandy Hopkinson, myself
Rob & James Ryan
Kate Ryan, Aimee & Nicole Smith, Brenda Fowler, Anne & James Perry.

Joe Pagano, Terry Lance, Graeme Clements
BJ Graham, Kerrie Hartin, Jan Lance, Jess Wales
James Perry, Jo, Rachel Goth, Marilyn Morgan Pam Schultz
Jeni Lewington, myself, Anne Perry, Karyn Pagano, ? , Susan Clements

FANS AND CELEBRATIONS

Fans at Performance of "Mother" starring beloved Noni Hazlehurst

Cruising with Fans

The Cruise

The Cruise

Foxy Lunch

High Tea with Fans

Christman Get Together

At Tim Draxl's Play

Natalie Hedington

What A Place to Call Home Means to Me

I didn't know that when I began watching A Place to Call Home (APTCH) when it first aired here in Australia back in 2013, that it would lead me to some of the best experiences and friendships.

I wasn't lucky enough to be able to share in the joy of saving the show, but I am and will be forever grateful to those who did. If it weren't for them, I would never have gotten the opportunity to meet the people I have (both fellow fans & cast members – one in particular) and share experiences with others.

APTCH for me is one of my go to shows for many things… writing student reports, if I'm feeling like a pick me up or I'm just up for a re-watch.

I remember watching season 6 as it aired on Foxtel in 2018, with a friend every Sunday. She'd come over to my place, one of us would've cooked dinner and we'd sit and watch it while enjoying the food and a glass or two of wine. When the final episode aired, I like many others I know, bawled my eyes out… I didn't want it to end, and I think to this day, I still haven't quite gotten over it!

I even visited some of the locations where it was filmed in rural NSW when my Dad and I were driving back to WA from QLD in 2019 and I visited some of the Sydney ones in 2020 when I took a trip over there.

I've also put a few friends in touch with it and they have enjoyed it as much as I have.

Even though I loved and valued every experience that I shared through the show, there are two things that stand out the most for me. They are making new friends, in particular Vanessa from the UK (a fellow Marta fan) and being very fortunate to organise and experience a Skype call for my Year 5/6 students with Marta Dusseldorp!

I'm not 100% sure on how my initial conversation with Vanessa began, but we both had something in common that assisted in our connection – all things Marta! Vanessa, like me, had discovered Marta, through APTCH. She has lived vicariously through all my "Marta experiences" and we've chatted about all kinds of things, sometimes for hours!

She has sent me surprise cards/gifts which have had me in tears (happy tears mind you) that someone, who I have never even met, would think to send me. She is one of the most thoughtful people I know and for that I am and always will be, eternally grateful… if it wasn't for A Place to Call Home it is highly likely that we would never have met!

How the Skype call happened is a long story, but so I'll try to keep it short!

It was International Women's Day, 2018 and the theme was "women that inspire you". I was a Year 5/6 teacher at the time, and I decided to set them a task of writing a speech about a woman that inspires them.

Now, the students I work with don't necessarily have the role models that most of us would. They also need a lot of modelling and help with what they need to do when completing activities.

Anyway, I decided that I would demonstrate what I wanted them to do by speaking about (to start with) and then by planning my speech on Marta. She inspires me in so many ways, but her work with refugees through UNHCR is one of the most inspiring.

When I had spoken to them about her (I had also given them several other prominent people both here in Australia and around the world) they had to choose who they were going to write about. I ended up having 2 of my girls come up to me and ask if they could write about Marta! How awesome is that?!

At first, I thought they may have been doing it to make it easier for themselves, as I had filled out the initial planning sheet, but I did tell them that they still had to complete everything themselves, as well as write their speech. I also asked them why and they both gave me legitimate answers that I couldn't say no, ha-ha!

That afternoon, I was so excited about what had happened that I tweeted about it, mentioned Marta in the tweet and she replied! The next day I showed my students, and they were so excited that she had replied that they wanted to meet her. Needless to say they were disappointed when I told them she didn't live in Perth so wouldn't be able to come into school.

It did get me thinking though… we live in the day and age of technology! Why could we not do some kind of video chat? So, I suggested this to my students and every one of them thought it weas a great idea and I reached out to Marta.

In the meantime, the students were working on their speeches, and I sent Marta a photo of the 2 girls typing them up and it was then that she mentioned the possibility of a Skype (she had read my tweet about it).

Well, long story short, we had the Skype call in the August of that year! My students (and I, of course) loved every minute of being able to speak to her about her work as an actor and specifically about APTCH (some of my students had watched the PG rated ones with me at lunch times), her role with UNHCR and Cancer Australia as well as several general questions.

I flew to Melbourne to see Marta in a play and met her in person for the first time, to thank her for what she did for my students and how much it meant. Even though she was exhausted I spent about 10 mins talking with her and handing over a gift that my students had made for her (and a few other bits & pieces – including copies of the girls' speeches). She came across just as I had imagined - she is a wonderful person with a beautiful soul, a fantastic role model. I hope she realised just how much her Skype call meant to me and my students and how appreciative we all were for her agreeing to it in the first place, as she didn't have to.

I've met her several times since then and she is always kind, friendly and accommodating, even when she is exhausted!

To this day I still feel blessed that she even took the time out of her busy schedule to speak to them and I know that there are a few who will remember it forever.

If it wasn't for A Place to Call Home, none of what I've spoken about in this piece would ever have happened and for that I am truly grateful!

The Skype call between Marta & my Year 5/6 students in 2018.

Both celebrating and commiserating the APTCH finale in 2018.

When I met Marta in 2018 in Melbourne to thank her for doing the Skype call. I look very different to how I look now! A lot of APTCH fans that know me, would never have seen me looking like this!

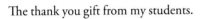

The thank you gift from my students.

My students Learning Journey with Marta (from beginning to end). Written by them, put together by me.

PART TWO: THE AUSTRALION STORY TRAVELS ACROSS THE GLOBE

FRAN SIMMONS

When I discovered A Place to Call Home, I was recovering from minor surgery in January 2016, and I happened to be watching BBC2 one afternoon. The TV program ended but as I was immobile, I sat watching what came on next. After the first 20 minutes I was absorbed – what was this show that had such fascinating characters and what were their stories? I was taken captive immediately, and I never looked back. I had to keep watching each afternoon as Season 1 played out on the TV in the afternoons and by the end of that Season I had already purchased Seasons 1-3 on DVD as I couldn't wait to continue the story of the Blighs!

I told my husband to watch the first episode with me and tell me what he thought. By the end of it he was asking if we could watch the next episode, and the next and the next and so on – he loved it too.

For me Sarah's story was the most fascinating and addictive. I couldn't compare my life at all to what we know she went through with the war, thinking she'd lost her husband, then finding him alive, falling in love with another man in the interim, her treatment at the hands of the Nazis and anti-Semitism pointed at her. But what I do feel I have in common with Sarah is that she didn't feel the need to behave a certain way or that she had to tell everyone about her past – it wasn't lying, just telling what she needed to, and when she needed to, to tell the people she felt she trusted enough to know those very private elements of her life. I think I felt that connection with Sarah's character as I recognize those characteristics in myself.

As the APTCH story developed, we became invested in a lot of the characters and wholeheartedly soaked up the family and the storylines – the sad moments, the happy moments and the occasional funny moment. The complex characters and the drama of reaching their end goal was riveting and as we moved into the next 3 seasons, I found myself wringing my hands waiting to see what some characters did next, or I dried a tear after the demise of intricate characters like Regina, and the heartbreaking death of Douglas. I also got frustrated and angry with some characters who were stubborn and how they couldn't open up to their loved ones or discuss their problems. I guess Bevan Lee intended us to feel a whole range of emotions and wrote the characters to evoke our emotions and passions for them.

Both my husband and I (and by now my teenaged son, Ben) were deeply engaged and captivated with the stunning scenery on the show – the outside scenes with the beautiful flora and fauna, the rockpool and water locations, the lush vegetation in some scenes and the dry arid grass in others – this intermingled with the sounds of the Australian birds, insects and other creature sounds that were encapsulated and replicated by the skilled visual and audio production team that created the show.

Before we had even finished watching the whole show, we were in love...with Australia! We started looking at the locations in and around Sydney and after a bit of research on flights and accommodation we decided we had to go to Australia and sample for ourselves the beauty and richness of the land that had struck us so much visually.

After watching the first Season of A Place to Call Home, I joined a couple of Facebook groups – the Save a Place to Call Home group (SAPTCH) and the (now defunct) International group. In amongst these groups, I found I had a lot in common with members who also were drawn to the show for a variety of reasons – but underlying all the reasons was the simple fact that we all loved the show! For me, I found I made a lot of new friends as well as co-admirers of the show – and I was even more blown away by finding that the people I was connecting with were all over the world. I began to make friends with Australians, Americans, Dutch, Swedish, Brits and other nationalities and through being members of the Facebook groups, we were able to chat about all sorts of topics about the show, the actors, the issues raised in the storylines, the scenery and so much more. With a good number of people, the connections and chats grew to be more than just "Facebook Friends," in quite a few instances we became firm friends and over the years since the show has aired, many of us have taken it upon ourselves to connect even more by meeting up – and that's no mean feat when people live thousands of miles away and on different continents!

Being part of the International group was great and gave me the impetus to organize 3 meet ups of group members – twice in Manchester and once in Southampton in the UK (our meet up in 2020 had to be cancelled due to Covid). Getting together with fellow APTCH fans has been amazing – again to consolidate friendships and also to have a good old gas about everything and anything! Some friends have come to all the meet ups in the UK and the medal for always making a huge effort goes to the "Crazy Dutch Ladies" (comprising of Nell, Marjolein and Marielle) who travel from the Netherlands specially to meet up. We have also been very lucky to have Gail travel from Israel to meet up with us in the UK and others who have travelled the length of the UK to join in. Our gatherings have been enhanced all the more when my co-administrator, Simon has been able to join us – it's always special to chat and catch up with the people who have been on the same journey regarding watching the show, then joining a Facebook group, becoming an Admin and then forming another, brand new group out of the ashes of the defunct International group. I had the pleasure of being able to travel to Boston in the USA in 2018 and met with my coadmins Marc, Amy, Catherine and other good APTCH stalwarts Donna and Jane as well as a couple of special New England CWA ladies! We ate, drank, chatted and laughed so much and told many stories of our APTCH experiences. I look forward to doing a return event or something similar with them all.

Back in June/July of 2018 the group that had brought so many of us together, the International group was archived due to "complications". I and a few of my close friends had decided that our friendships and community of people who shared so much together in the International group should try and continue the band of people in a new Facebook group and that there was still so much for us to continue in a group based on friendships and community as well as having the show as the basis of its raison d'être. On the 22nd of July 2018, myself, Simon, Marc, Catherine, Amy and June began our new group – APTCH Community Group – with our philosophy being Bevan Lee's words - "Friendships, warmth, decency and caring are what get you through the hard times." The introduction to our group on Facebook says: "Our APTCH Community was borne as a fresh perspective of our shared love of A Place to Call Home. This group was created jointly and equally by people who have formed friendships as a result of the TV show. The Community we would like to share with others is one which began with APTCH and now spills over and beyond the show itself and will perpetuate beyond the final episode."

When we started the group, we decided we weren't interested in membership numbers – it was all about friends chatting and enjoying discussing things from the show that affected them or asking questions or needing help. We started as 6 friends and as time has gone by (over 2 years in fact!) we have been lucky to have over 1,600 others come and join us in our Community. We've had a lot of cross over with members from the SAPTCH group with whom we have a great relationship – the Aussies that saved the show are held in great esteem because if it weren't for them, the show would never have continued to 6 seasons, and we probably wouldn't be where we are with our group and I wouldn't be writing this! So, a big thank you always goes out to the SAPTCHers, some of whom I consider to be good friends of mine too now.

In August 2017 I, along with my husband Roger and son Ben, travelled to Australia for a 3 week "Holiday of a Life-time!" And it truly was. From the fantastically cosmopolitan cities like Sydney and Melbourne, to the endless coast-line with beautiful sandy beaches interrupted by sporadic, craggy, rocky lookouts onto the Tasman Sea and equally beautiful National forests oozing with many different species of gum, acacia and pine trees. How exciting it was to spot kangaroos and wallabies when driving through the National parks and amusing also to find them hopping around in front of your hotel room when you stayed in a town. Waking up to the singing of galahs, kookaburras, magpies and currawong really got you into the feel of being in Australia and was reminiscent of the sounds we heard on APTCH. We delighted in the contrast of freezing mornings in view of the snowcapped Snowy Mountains and shaded our eyes to see the hazy vistas over the enormous, sun-drenched gorges in the Blue Mountains. There were so many highlights for us on our trip that we felt we had only scratched the surface of what Australia is. What we did realize and understood from our visit, is how very welcoming, friendly and helpful Australians are. This Aussie warmth has been evident not only on our trip, but also from the Aussies in the SAPTCH group and the Community Group. That many amongst them will go out of their way to help us Internationals, is a testament to Australian hospitality. There are some Aussies in particular that have met with international visitors, given them hospitality, accommoda-tion, taken them on excursions and organized events for them to meet other Aussies, see APTCH locations and given much needed help and advice. Once again, I applaud them for their community spirit and for being great Aussies!

Our own experience of meeting some of these great Aussies, was when we were in the Blue Mountains. It was a great privilege to meet with Brenda and spend some time with her and her husband. As we had travelled to Australia in August, our timetable didn't fall well with the filming of APTCH, so we weren't able to go and see any of that process as other international travelers had, but nevertheless, we were very happy to have met up with Brenda. And later, when we were back in Sydney, we met up with a group of SAPTCHers including the marvelous Margaret and my good friend Lyndal and her husband Stuart (both of whom I've met with a couple of times in London due to connecting with APTCH!) It was lovely to put names to new faces and have a good chat over lovely food with the magnificent Sydney Harbour Bridge as a backdrop.

As mentioned, we travelled to Australia when APTCH wasn't filming so we were not able to visit the studio or see any filming. What we were able to do, however, was visit several locations that were used during the filming of the series. I had bought an invaluable Location guide written by Jeni Lewington, and we used that to visit numerous locations in and around Sydney. We went to the Argyle Stairs, Picton Railway Viaduct, Menangle, Thirlmere Station as well as numerous houses used for locations in Merriman St, Lower Fort St and a couple of the churches also used in the show.

Once we knew we would be near Camden, I had to make sure we went past Camelot – APTCH's "Ash Park". I wanted to at least try and get a photo or two from the road. We drove to Kirkham and pulled up a little way past the gates to Camelot. Ben and I walked to the gates and tried to take photos of the house in the distance at the end of the driveway – it was an awesome moment to stand there where they had filmed the show and many of the cast and crew had been creating the show we had come to love. We were on the threshold of being a part of it all and we were giddy at seeing Ash Park in the distance! Then, we had to stand aside as a car drove up to the gate and a lady got out to open the gate. I apologized if we were in the way and said we had come from the UK to visit and that we loved APTCH and just wanted to take a couple of photos. It turned out the lady was the owner of Camelot- Rachel. She chatted with us for a while then suggested we could get better pictures of the front entrance of the house if we went down the side road. So, we thanked her and duly went to the side road which was where you look down onto the front door of Ash Park! Unfortunately, the undergrowth was quite tall and as Ben tried to move foliage aside to see the house, a dog started barking at him from in the grounds of Camelot. Ben tried to get a couple of photos, but not very successfully, and then we heard a voice call out from an opened, arched window in Camelot, "Why don't you come down the driveway and take as many photos of the house as you'd like?" It was Rachel and she very kindly offered to let us onto the property and drive down the driveway and up to the house! Well, it was more than a dream come true to be driving down that famous driveway and up to the stables that we had seen in so many of the scenes in APTCH. Our hearts were thumping with what we were taking in – the stables, the guesthouse, the front lawns and then around to the front of the house to see the two lions sitting guarding the front entrance to "Ash Park".

Up close the house is stunningly elegant with the shuttered, arched windows and the balconied ground and first floor overlooking the vast lawns and gardens. You cannot help but look up at the roof and the cone shaped rooftop amongst the red bricks of the house and huge chimneys together with the grey tiles which give the house its dignified, serene look. We wandered around the outside of the house taking lots of photos from the various places of scenes we had seen in the show – all the time pinching ourselves in disbelief that we were so lucky to have been invited to do so. It was so unexpected, and I have to say that this was the moment that was the cherry on the top of our amazing visit to Australia. There are many things I take away, not only from our trip to Australia when we were blown away by the warmth, generosity and kindness of the people we met there, but as I go full circle as to how this came about - meeting these wonderful people and befriending people in the groups and having fantastic experiences as well as seeing such breathtaking places – it all comes back to one thing. A Place to Call Home.

I am eternally grateful that I was in the right place at the right time to enable me to start my initial steps on this journey and to meet people that am happy to call friends now. In these strange times when we haven't been able to travel or visit friends and family, it has been a heartwarming, uplifting thing to be able to go to our Facebook group and chat and raise spirits, or to Zoom chat with a group from across the continents and discuss the show or life events and have fun and laugh too. Although the show has ended, we can be grateful that it lives on in those of us who partake in the groups. I am so glad and proud to be able to be part of such a special community of people that puts out the familiar Welcome Mat to anyone who wishes to join us.

CATHERINE CHENEY
The APTCH Effect

I discovered A Place To Call Home on Public Television, one afternoon in late 2016. I had been homebound for several weeks, following a fall which shattered my kneecap (I wish I could claim a climbing accident, but it sadly, it was the result of slipping in a puddle of water next to a frozen food case in the grocery store). Up until my convalescence, I honestly did not watch a lot of TV, other than a few favorite series. But this one hooked my within minutes.

I don't recall which episode it was, though I'm fairly certain it was from S1; there may have been a couple aired back-to-back. Soon I was frantically searching for more information about this program, and how I could see more of it. That lead to an Acorn TV subscription and before long, I was searching for fan groups where I could *talk* about this brilliant series.

By February 2017, I was a member of 2 FB groups (APTCH Int'l and the Save APTCH groups) and was discussing plots, characters and costume with folks from around the globe. S4 had aired in Australia late in 2016, and I had the pleasure of watching it roll out, week by week, on Acorn. By March, I had even entered a fan fiction contest sponsored by the Int'l group, and then reached well out of my comfort zone to RSVP to a group brunch in NYC in June, at the home of Donna Divine.

June came, and I still was recovering from my injury, but off I went on the train to visit with people I had never met before (on a side note, that was also Gay Pride Day in NYC, and there was also a Yankees home game – the train in from Connecticut was standing room only – about 45% Yankee fans, 45% Parade participants, and 10% amused onlookers enjoying the interaction between the groups).

To this day, I am in frequent communication with several people I met that day. We have meet in person on several occasions and have some pretty active group chats in Facebook Messenger. The highlight of that brunch, though, was learning that I had won 2nd prize in the Fan Fiction contest and having that announced (via a taped video message) by none other than Bevan Lee!

As the Facebook groups grew, I had another, more local occasion to meet with some avid fans right in Connecticut. On the coldest day in January 2018, 4 of us met at a tearoom in central Connecticut. (Donna was planning on being part of this meet-up but was unable to join us at the last minute). By the time we said goodbye that day, we arranged to meet again, and our own version of the CWA was born. That is – the Connecticut Women's Association. We continue to meet in various combinations, to this day.

ADVENT OF COMMUNITY
Catherine Cheney Nov. 2020

As I mentioned in my prior essay, the APTCH International Facebook group opened a whole new world for me. It was notable for the Administrator's (I'll call her A) access to the founders of the Save APTCH group, which helped her get access to the creator and cast of the series, so there were Skype conversations with cast members, and contests with prizes of themed goods not available in the US. And there were friendships. In April of 2018, the CWA (Connecticut Women's Association), planned a get together, and A said she would come in from NYC to attend. Amy Tatem-Bannister (a page Moderator) agreed to come from the Boston area, and Fran Simmons (another Moderator), devised a Trivia Quiz for the gathering. A brought along some 'swag', which we auctioned off with the proceeds going to a local homeless shelter in recognition of Noni Hazlehurst's role in the play "Mother". And the gathering also served as a send-off to A, who was headed for Australia.

It is difficult to explain all this without talking – unkindly, but truthfully – about A, and I am not going to do so here, but suffice it to say that there were increasing tensions between her and her Moderators (and others she asked to organize various things). More tensions arose while she was Down Under, and these tensions threatened to alienate all associated from the core members of the Save group, as well as cast members.

For some time, there was a Private Message group of A's 'minions' where we shared concerns and frustrations about what we were asked (demanded) to do and forbidden to do. We found we were being dismissed by our association with A, by the very people in Australia who had much to share with fans in other countries around the world. And so we began talking about a breakout group. It was not an easy decision – it felt disloyal and dismissive of a person who had done so much to bring us together. But the Int'l group was becoming less interactive and more autocratic; questions were being directed to A that she ignored, and it was uncomfortable. We set up a dummy page to talk about ideas, and after numerous pep talks, we launched the APTCH Community Group in July 2018. The biggest difference is that there are 6 Admins for the group – not one Admin and several Moderators. Our "About" page reflects our reasons for staring this new group, and I think we have remained true to this mantra.

"Friendships, warmth, decency and caring are what get you through the hard times" - Bevan Lee.

Our APTCH Community was borne as a fresh perspective of our shared love of A Place to Call Home. This group was created jointly and equally by people who have formed friendships as a result of the TV show. The Community we would like to share with others is one which began with APTCH and now spills over and beyond the show itself and will perpetuate beyond the final episode.

We will share our common interests that endeared us to the show - the characters, the cast, the social issues, lifestyles, locations, socialising, music, family - the list is endless.

Our APTCH Community FB Group will embrace pastures new as well as old. We will continue to champion Bevan Lee's sentiments of using ourselves as "a conduit to encourage warmth, decency, love and empathy." And let us surround ourselves with those who do likewise.

*The Founders and Administrators of the APTCH Group are:
Fran Simmons & Simon Collins in the UK.
Amy Tatem-Bannister & Catherine Cheney on the east coast of the US.
Marc Kenig on the west coast of the US; and
June Anderson in Australia

We communicate regularly through FB chat; we've Zoomed, and we have all (I believe) met at least one of our co-Admins. In October of 2018 we had a meet-up in Boston, Massachusetts with Amy, Catherine, Fran (visiting from the UK0, and Marc (who timed his trip from California to coincide with Fran's visit. We were joined by family, other Community members (including Donna Divine and Jane Sullivan (all the way from Georgia!)) and shared an afternoon of shenanigans and laughs…all due to a little Australian period drama. Whodathunkit????

VAL HOBBS

I first came across 'A Place to Call Home' when I was on a three month visit to Australia from the UK in 2013. My daughter was expecting her second child and needed Nana to come and look after no. 1, while she had no. 2.

I arrived at the end of May and one afternoon my daughter said to me, ' Oh you might like this Mum, as you are a fan of historical dramas', I am a keen fan of Downton Abbey! And I sat down to watch while my new grandson napped on my shoulder! And I loved it from the first episode I saw, which was episode 2 of Series 1. Dear Elizabeth Bligh irritated about the mysterious [as she saw it] Sarah, Olivia in the early stages of pregnancy and Doris Collins fishing for information in Sarah's room.

I saw almost all the rest of that series and then came home to the UK. About two years later APTCH popped up on British afternoon TV and to my delight there were three series waiting for me there! And I watched them all on catch up TV.

I didn't spend much time on Facebook, and never thought about looking for a support group until 2019 when I was unwell and home for long periods and not able to move about much . I got an Amazon Prime subscription and found all the series on there! Oh joy! I have now watched them all sequentially three times! And my husband is a fan too. At a time when I was feeling 'a bit rough' as Roy would put it, I watched APTCH and it made me feel closer to my daughter in Australia in a variety of ways – the background of bird noises so familiar in Australia, but not heard in the UK, the wonderful views of parts of Sydney, the beautiful scenery and great camera shots of creeks, fields, Sydney

Harbour, the old buses and no opera house! The accents of course brought my son in law and his family to mind and set in the 50's the wonderful costumes took me back to my childhood when my mother dressed like Regina, Sarah and Anna. I was also struck by the attention to detail in costume, household items, the wonderful cars and Frankie J Holden, grinning out of his battered old Truck with Lucky lounging on the flatbed. I had a soft spot for Roy as my maiden surname was Briggs, I was born 1951, so not quite old enough to be of an age with Dawn's daughter Emma.

Thank you to SAPTCH for saving the show and getting it continued for three more series! It has given me and all the friends I have alerted to it on UK re-showings a great deal of pleasure and enjoyment.

MARTINE STOUTEN-MULDER
My Story; A Place To Call Home.

My Story; A Place To Call Home.

This show has changed my life in a good way. Before I found the program, I found very little I wanted or liked to do or put energy in. Flipping through all the tv channels one very early Saturday morning; i saw Brett Climo in the 6th or 7th episode of the first season...I just stared at the screen,... thinking back to my younger years, when i was watching my favorite show The Flying Doctors staring Brett Climo...

I never expected to like a show as much as The Flying Doctors but I soon found myself holding as much love for APTCH as I did for the earlier show.

With some help from a friend, I actually wrote a personal letter to Andrew McFarlane one of the stars of Flying Doctors. I always found help in this TV series in coping with all sort of lifetime challenges. When life was hard, watching a movie/other show he was in or an FD episode made me feel better. I actually read on his fan page about his role in Place To Call Home and was determined to see the program.

Seeing one episode encouraged me to want to see more. Brousing the internet, I soon found a Dutch fanclub of APTCH and from its very first activity, I found other friends for life: Marjolein Nell Martine R. Dianne and Marielle. A friendship was born that has lasted to this day.

How Nell and I met for the first time I will never forget in my life... It still makes me smile and laugh when I think about that evening. Although we had trouble finding our way to the first gathering in Zoetermeer, we found one another. We call ourselves the "Crazy" Dutch Girls (named by Marjolein) and are the best friends you could have. Im so proud to be one of them.

I knew about the intention to end the Series after the second Season. We supported the the SAPTCH group in Australia and joined their Facebook efforts. I am so glad it was saved.

I very much enjoyed Season 3 particularly because it introduced our Famous Doctor Fox, Henry Fox !!! The first scene with Elisabeth was so amazing, and cute to see. (Coincidentally, on 6th september 2016, I began a personal journey, diagnosed with a Diabetic feed and a close call almost losing a toe. Lucky for me, it did not happen at the time.) Having to stay at home, I watched the show. Searching the internet, I found the Foxy fanpage of Tim Draxl, became a member and never regreted that decision. Such an amazing person. Loving his music, when im happy or not his music or seeing him on stage or screen it helps get through a day or week ,...

This year i was able to meet Tim by a zoommeeting. It was so much fun, and I hope that he will sing/record that song together with Dominic (Harry Polson) and David (James Bligh) ...

Can't forget to say that I'm grateful meeting so many friends here in these groups, especially Dawn (and her family) my best Foxy Friend for life. It's special to have a friend who means so much to you. I am lucky: I didn't just find a friend, I found a whole family of friends who became like a family for me. While I can't name you all just know you have a place in my heart. It doesn't matter where you are from or what you do we all share the love of our show.

Thank you from the bottom of my heart Bevan Lee who wrote the story, the actors for playing their roles so amazing. all the people we dont get to see behind the scenes, to make it happen.

with you all there I can say I've found my place to call home

one day I will hope to see you all.

MARJOLEIN HUL
The Crazy Dutch girls!

Hi, my name is Marjolein and I live in this really small country in Europe, the Netherlands.

I saw APTCH for the first time in July 2015. It appears to be on public tv every weekday and started on Friday. The time slot was around dinnertime, so I recorded it.

I have a great love for Australia in general; Aboriginal art, and Aussie tv shows, ever since I was a kid. When i watched APTCH on Saturday morning, I was hooked after 20 min as Sarah talks back to Elizabeth when she wants to examine her on the deck of the ship. After I had finished the episode, I wanted more so I binged the first 2 seasons online that weekend!! And of course, I followed it every weekday on Dutch tv. I googled the show and found the Facebook groups. I learned a lot about the show, the characters, the actors and the savers, so- called SAPTCH-ers. What a story that is! I wish I could have made a contribution as well. By the time i became aware of the show it was already saved. The only thing I could do was to buy all the DVDs to support and I did.

On Facebook I became friends with a few SAPTCHters and a lot of other fans of the show. Also, I saw fellow Dutch fans on Facebook and together with one of them i founded the Dutch fan group and made the local newspaper. We came together at a meeting with Dutch fans and shared our love and knowledge of the show. That was great. At that meeting I became friends with a few Dutch girls. We kept in contact and had our little meet ups somewhere in the Netherlands. There are six of us and we became really close as we speak of our love for Australia and the tv shows. We have this chat group going on all day, every day!

As i became Facebook friends with other fan fans around the world, i would like to visit them in the meetings they were organising. That's how three of us Dutch girls ended up in the UK to meet some fans overt here! I now could combine my love of the show with my love to travel! Also this lady from Israël was there. Gail. How i loved it. We spend a couple of days together with the four of us and joined the meeting with the UK fans. There were true friend-ships formed.

When i got my two kittens, , I named them after my two favorite characters: Jack and Caro. You can follow them on Instagram. (And I am a big Regina-fan but I have only two kittens to name)

I had planned a trip to Israel in 2018 with friends when I learned there was this last gala on "Ash park". One Dutch girl was going and I was more and more thinking of going. That meant two more weeks of leave. I talked to my boss and I got permission!! So, I went to Israel first and when I came in Jerusalem, i saw Gail again. We spend the day together. My other friends went to a museum and Gail and I did some mischief in the city. Later that day my other friends joined us.

When I got home from Israel, I had to pack my bags again. Together with another Dutch lady (Nell) ,we went to Sydney. Then I started to call us The Crazy Dutch Girls. We travel the world for our beloved show, how crazy is that? In Sydney we met a lot of our Facebook friends in real life. I felt deeply connected immediately. We spend a weekend in Camden, did two days of location tours and oh my, what fun we had. How honored we were to be "on the holy ground of Ash park" and could walk around. We sent pictures to our Dutch girls back home all the time so they could join the things we did. We also met new people. I've enjoyed every minute of it. In those two weeks we did also a lot of meetings with friends, made new ones, saw a play with Tim Draxl, did some tourist stuff and so on. I have a copy of Jeni Lewington's book and we took it as our tour guide in Sydney, especially in the Rocks. We had great fun and it was sad to leave as we had to go home.

When I got home, we planned a sleepover at one of the other Dutch girls houses and had a videocall with a few Aussies as they were having farewell picnics in a lot of places. For us it was in the middle of the That didn't bother us. We had fun. When i saw my friends over there I started to think: I want to go again.

In the meantime, I had meet ups in Amsterdam with fellow fans who are from Australia and were on a cruise that ended in Amsterdam.

The Crazy Dutch Girls went to meet ups in Belgium and UK again. So much fun to talk to people with the same interests. And..... I want to make a trip to Australia that I wanted to make ever since I was 14 yrs. old. I started dreaming of that................

I only have a few weeks off a year. I talked to my boss again. I wanted to save my six weeks of leave the whole year and take it in December 2019 and January 2020. Guess what? I've got permission again! Do I want to go by myself? I asked Nell if she wants to join me again. She did. We planned our whole trip. We had a lot of fun doing so and when our itinerary was complete, we let our friends down under know.

We had a great welcome, stayed at friends' houses and had meet ups in a lot of places. I felt back home again. We saw a play with Noni Hazelhurst and she had coffee with us afterwards, we visited Jack Ellis' his studio and bought some paintings, and we went to Frankie J Holden's caravan park and were invited by him to join one of his music sessions. We covered half of the continent in those six weeks! We did a lot of driving, had domestic flights and spent New Year's Eve in Sydney. What a dream holiday! And so many friends who were somehow part of it.

Although there were these terrible bushfires, we could still manage to make our trip as planned. What a journey we had.

Now I am home in my small country. Feeling homesick to Australia.

But who could have thought that one tv show had so much impact in my life and let me make my dream (-trip) come true?

Thank you cast and friends helping it happen!

(And when this stupid COVID is gone.......expect me again)

Me, at Ash park.

NELL VAN DE GRAAF
DOUBLE DUTCH

A few years ago, I was at a birthday party and one of the other guests was talking with me about my holiday trips to Australia. I was there in 2010 and 2012 with my twins sister on a road trip up the east coast. She told me that one of our television companies broadcasts a series about a nurse who was back in Australia after 20 years and how wonderful the episodes were. So, the next day I looked and was hooked on it right away.

On the internet, I saw there were Facebook groups in Holland and in Australia. Anton van Dijken was chief of the Dutch group and there was a meeting soon. I went to the meeting and find some ladies who became friends.

In the meantime, e we connected with groups in the UK and Belgium.

There was a meeting in Manchester and the "Crazy "Dutch Girls took a plane to the meeting and became friends with the English group. we had a lovely time that weekend.

Antwerp is not so far so we also met the Belgian fans.

In de meanwhile season 2 was broadcast and we heard that there was a protest meeting and a letter writing campaign in Australia to pressure channel 7 to make more APTCH.

Then, the garden parties were held, and I was envious. Australia was 24 hours by plane, I could not come in time.

Then, in 2018 the last garden party would be held. Through the Australian site I asked if it possible to fly in and be a guest on the party. But there was a problem: I had an infected jaw, and the dentist forbid me to fly. I had an operation and lots of antibiotics. In September I got permission to fly. In the meantime, one of the other members of the Dutch group asked me if I wanted to go. I told her my problem and after a few days we spoke about the trip. Marjolein Hul and I booked a flight to Sydney.

and a car a hotel and informed the Australian group that we would arrive a week before the party.

We flew to Sydney and met all the members of the Australian group and made a lot of friends. All were so lovely and there was hospitality.

It was special to be at Camelot in the garden of the mansion called Ash Park where the series was filmed. They even gave us a tour of the neighbourhood of Camden, and we saw a lot of places used in the series, We had a marvelous time and made a lot of new friends. The Australians made me feel like I was one of them. Brenda Fowler, Margaret Jackson, and Peter Vernon made arrangements for us. We had lunches, tea parties and they showed us around.

After 2 weeks we had to go back to Holland because I have to be at home because my first grandchild was born. And we had to work to earn money for the next trip!

After a year we flew back to Sydney for a trip of 7 weeks. And all the friends were gathered and gave us an awesome beginning of the trip. We went to see Noni Hazelhurst in The Beauty Queen of Lenane

She was awesome and after the play we had a meeting with her. I cannot express the feelings of joy and happiness that she gives me. Such a humble, down- to -earth woman.

The next day we met Jack Ellis, another member of the APTCH cast, and a marvelous painter. I brought a painting home that is on my wall in my living room.

Marjolein and I went to ULURU, Adelaide, Melbourne, and in every town, they had organized a lunch or tea party. We met a lot more members of the APTCH groups. And it felt like homecoming. On the trip we slept in the houses of Katarina, Ann, Lucy, and others. There was such hospitality. We made friends for a lifetime.

On the way back to Sydney we made a stop at Tatra beach. There we met Franky J. Holden who was so surprised that we made a trip all the way from Holland to meet him. Later on I asked him in a Zoom meeting If he knew the impact that the series had worldwide.

The only one we did not meet was Marta Dusseldorp, the one with the Dutch heritage. That will be next time. We will go than to Tasmania.

I cannot fully express my feelings and the amount I've learned from APTCH. The series taught me a lot about rural Australia in the 50s and many things about Jewish beliefs. For me it was a win-win situation, the friends I've got on the other side of the world who will be there when I land on their soil and who can visit me when they are land here.

Gail Siegel

Like any good story, you start at the beginning. My name is Gail Siegel and I live in Israel. In the late 1960s, my family planned to immigrate to Australia. My mom had a job lined up and it sounded like it would be a great adventure. However, things changed, and we moved to upstate New York instead.

The desire to go to Australia never lessened for my sister and me. She would surf the internet looking for any Australian TV shows. A few years ago, while I was on vacation in Scotland, she said to check out this show about a Jewish nurse in Inverness, Australia. I tried to watch on my Kindle, but the screen was too small, and I didn't try again once I got home.

A few months later, YES TV started showing the show and I decided to watch on the TV, which had a bigger screen than the Kindle. Well, you guessed it, I was hooked. (I should mention that YES TV carried the show on video on demand (VOD) every day and had all the seasons. You can still find it on VOD, just not all the seasons) After season 2 aired and the show was cancelled by Channel 7, some faithful fans in Australia decided to hold 'protest' picnics. (Their stories will be found in another place in this book.)

Again, my sister told me that there is a group on Facebook called the Save A Place To Call Home Group and that I should join to check out the picnics. So, I did. I remember waking up in the middle of the night to check the videos and photos that were being posted. I was excited for those participating when the cast showed up at some of the picnics. Wow, I thought, these people are making a stand and letting their voices be heard. The cast were so appreciative that they showed up and have shown up at further SAPTCHer events.

At that time, I didn't know how my life would change. Somewhere along the way, I decided to treat myself to a trip to Australia for my 60th birthday. This was a dream of a lifetime for me as I would be seeing the country my family almost moved to many years before. My adventure began at Brisbane Airport when Jeni Lewington picked me up. On that first day, I was thrilled to hold a koala, another lifetime dream.

Myself, Mars Browne ad Jeni Lewington at Glass House Mountains, Queensland

From that point on, I began to meet others of the group who saved our beloved show as my trip took me from Brisbane to Sydney to Camden, where a lot of filming took place, and finished in Melbourne. What is great about this group is that, even though we haven't met in person, we know one another's faces and names. When meeting some SAPTCHers for the first time after a train ride, organised by Jeni, instead of being introduced to everyone, you simply went up to them and started talking to them. You knew who everyone was. It was a great feeling!

There were many highlights of my trip, including meeting other fans and having great tour guides (Jeni, Brenda Fowler, Margaret Jackson), AND meeting some of the cast as well as the creator and writer of A Place to Call Home, Bevan Lee. Without him, there would not have been a show, the fans would not have met, and I don't know if I ever would have made it to Australia.

Meeting more fans after the train ride: Jeni Lewington, Jess Wales, Brenda Fowler, Nicole Anne, Josephine Edwards, Anne Kimber, Dolores Ryan, Cassandra Graham

No trip is complete without a visit to Manly. With Annette Van Lierop, myself, Josephine Edwards, Brenda Fowler, Margaret Jackson, and Joel.

I joined another related Facebook group and through chats 'met' Marjolein Hul, from the Netherlands, and Donna Robinson Divine, from New York. We started connecting outside the group. Both visited me in Israel, and I have spent time with Donna in New York. I hope one day soon to visit Marjolein and the rest of the "Crazy Dutchies" in the Netherlands. Marjolein and I met the first time in Manchester, U.K. for one of the APTCH Community Group meetups. I also met Fran Simmons, Jenni Rigby, Saffron Darling, Neil Van de Graf and Mariele Vijn. There were others whom I met as well, but the names are foggy.

I met Donna for the first time in New York while visiting my sister.

Donna and I on a blustery day in Jerusalem.

Marjolein Hul and Gail Siegel in Jerusalem

Manchester meet-up with Marjolein Hul, Mariele Vijn, Fran Simmons, Saffron Darling, Jenni Rigby, and others

What started out as watching a TV show, turned into having friends around the world. I look forward to returning to Australia one day and having that cup of coffee with Margaret Jackson. Until then, I hope to travel closer to home and see my friends in the Netherlands and the UK and wherever else I may go.

How did the show affect me? I learned a little about the history of Australia from the 1950s of their treatment of Indigenous and gay people, what people thought about Jews, about the female concentration camp called Ravensbruck, and how people can change. Lifelong friendships have come out of the show.

Thank you, Bevan Lee, for creating the show, and the wonderful cast who portrayed their parts so well, so much so that in seasons 1 and 2 we hated Elizabeth, but by seasons 3, 4, 5 and 6 we loved her. Regina is another story! Thank you to the fans who saved the show and for all of you who are part of the SAPTCH and Community Groups, may you have your own adventures.

SUSAN LOBEL

About 3 years ago, my beloved cockatiel Roger passed, very unexpectedly. He was my very favorite bird in my 25-year holistic exotic bird rescue -- ,a joy, and one of the great loves of my life. No one would believe his intelligence and sensitivity. He is still missed. Around that time, APTCH was on my queue on Netflix DVD, and for a few months I looked at the summary and was looking forward to what I thought might be a very interesting story. Well, when I finally saw it, I was immediately "hooked" by the storyline, acting, the mood, the music, the plot the scenery, and the props. It helped me get through my intense grief regarding Roger. I watched it continually for 2 years straight. All I can say that when you find the perfect recipe for a perfect series, this is it for me and I will never forget this experience. In addition, I greatly appreciate the honor of hosting a column for the past year and a half, which I started, mainly to keep the memory of this show alive. I am very grateful to the group for the immense participation and to the administration for allowing me to do. Even though I will never get over Roger, this show made my life bearable. With many thanks.

JANICE CHAPPIE

Is there a place to call home?
Yes, it's a house that turns into a home
With unrest from the start
Living in Ash Park
So much drama
For family and friends
And so much heart
Living in Ash Park
We love the drama
We love the cast
We wanted it not to end
A love that will not part
For us and Ash Park

The very first scene where Brett Climo/George comes out of his cabin on the ship and meets Sarah for the first time I knew this would be a romance I would want to follow. Then there was the music which really sealed it for me. Great tunes from the fifties. Beside the story of George and Sarah was the rest of the story which included: World War 2, Nazis camps and the treatment of Jews and others in those horrible camps. Homosexuality and how it was treated and how it played out in that time frame. How women were treated as second class citizens and how two strong women, Sarah and Elizabeth fought to be heard. Most important to me was how George could be a genuine kind and gentle soul with all the lives that affected him. How he grew and how he became stronger while still helping others like his sister and his children. This drama made a major difference in my life. It gave me peace and enjoyment when I really needed those things. It has and still is a great passion in my life and I must include all the friends I have made in our continued support of A Place To Call Home.

EILEEN CONTENTO

Being quarantined with a housebound husband, APTCH has been my selfish indulgence. I have watched it over and over and have many favorite scenes, mostly those including Jack and Caroline. I also love Noni's expressions, watching her character breaking out from her golden handcuffs that was her old life into a modern woman helping others was so positive to see. You're never too old to evaluate your life's path and make a course correction.

Joining the fan groups has also expanded my world for the better. I have met and talked to people from England, Australia, New Zealand, Canada and Texas. I have read Hagit's poetry, seen Frida's woven shawls, talked elections with Brandy and drooled over Fran's calendar to name only a few. The show is great, but the people are even better.

RONNI KRASNOW

By almost every measure, 2020 was a horrific year— global pandemic, unfathomable death, unemployment, economic ruin and political chaos.

But I was one of the lucky ones. I held on to my job, and my friends and family remained healthy. So, for me, 2020 will always be the year I discovered A Place to Call Home.

By the end of March, about three weeks into quarantine, I was desperate for something new to binge. I saw that Acorn had a 30 -day free trial, so I figured there was no harm in trying it. The show was one of the first choices listed under "popular series". I thought the title sounded horribly cheesy, but when I saw there were six seasons, I decided it would keep me occupied for a while. I was wrong, because once I started watching I couldn't stop. From the moment in the first episode when Sarah's mother said, "take your Jew name and go", I knew this was no ordinary series. I was captivated by the story, the costumes, and especially Marta's incredible performance as Sarah. I finished the entire series in less than two weeks.

When I was done, I was DESPERATE to talk to someone about it, but I didn't know anyone who had even heard of it, so I logged onto Facebook, found our community, and now my life will never be the same. I learned about the incredible history of the show and got my hands on everything I could that Marta had done. After a few weeks, I felt more comfortable with posting and commenting in the group. I did the character study posts each week, and then volunteered to do the weekly episode discussion posts. I started "meeting" people from Australia and all over the world. Some of them have become friends I now can't imagine my life without. Brenda Fowler and Suzanne Walters moved heaven and earth to get a signed program from Marta, and they've never even met me. Fran Simmons has been so generous in sending me shows that aren't available in the US At this point, we only know each other virtually, but now traveling to Australia to meet everyone and see Marta on stage is the number one thing on my bucket list.

COVID-19 took so much from so many, but it ended up giving me something for which I will be forever grateful.

HAGIT CARMEL

I joined the Facebook group "APTCH Community - A Place To Call Home" in June 2020.

Since then, I put up a poem, each week for each episode.

This group along with the characters of APTCH are such an inspiration.

A few poems in my first poetry book were born here in this group, in English. Later I translated them to Hebrew and my editor decided that they should appear in the book.

So, among other obvious reasons to love A Place to Call Home, here is another one!

My first poetry book in a foreign language is a journey in history.

It starts with a mysterious woman who is coming back to Australia wishing to find A PLACE TO CALL HOME.

Watching her in the first episode, gazing to the horizon while standing on deck, inspired me to start my tradition to write my weekly poem.

Here are the poems of the first two seasons with short introductions for context when needed. There is one bonus in the end.

<u>Haunted by Past and Fighting for Sacred Privacy</u>
Aunt Peg brought a 'WELCOME' mat to her niece,
But demons were stronger, chasing her peace.
She once shot a friend, and then a wounded horse.
To save their souls, she shot them both.
She had a secret; she had a different name.
She knew a secret about a certain man.
But when a town crier her privacy invaded
The little trust she had immediately was faded.

.'How will I find you now?'

The story of Sarah and Rene is revealed to us in small pieces, throughout three seasons: In the first season we learn about them being arrested and about Lorca's poetry book (Yom Kippur episode), and how they met (Sarah's mother death episode). In season two we learn about Sarah's trauma after she found out Rene was dead (James's release from hospital episode). Season three is their second life together, "Til Death Do Us Part".

This is their story:

It was a heartbreaking story
Love of second sight
They met in Paris then in Spain
She converted to marry
Then the war came.

She was standing in the station
Waiting for his train
Saw some scarecrow faces
But her husband never came.
She gave a piercing scream
Fell into the darkness
Tried to start again
Happy ever after.

When happiness emerged
He came back from the dead
She left her second love
Not knowing what's ahead.

Back to Paris there he was
Injured in his brain
He joined her to the place called home
She was devoted to his care.

They planned a future with her child
Starting a new leaf
But for two fighters came again
A new catastrophe.

She lost him once before
She grieved for him for such long time
And now she didn't really know
How to do it a second time.

And there she opened Lorca's book
And read for one last time
The poem of him going off,
Covered up by endless shroud,
Empty to the stars.

VANESSA VERLINDEN
My APTCH story

It's December 2017 and a UK TV channel called Drama, is advertising a series called "A Place to Call Home", to start in early January 2018. I love period dramas, and this looked interesting, so I put it on recording, as I would not be back in the UK until at least the first week of January.

We're a few weeks into January and I decide to go through all my recordings done while I was away for the holidays. I came to APTCH and by then it had already recorded 4 episodes. I was uhm-ing and ah-ing, wondering if I could be bothered to start watching, as it would take me about 3 hours to watch those, and I just wasn't sure about it. But then I thought, "meh, let's watch the first episode, and if I don't like it, I'll just delete the rest of the episodes and not bother".

Oh. My. Word.

I needn't have worried. Barely a few minutes in, I was already intrigued by a very determined Sarah walking up to her mother's door and being out again within seconds. But then, wow, the show down with Elizabeth, and then the show down with her mother. I was hooked! Funnily enough, just that week or so, I had read an article about women who convert to Judaism changing their names. When Aunt Peg called her Bridget/Sarah, and the fact that she'd been in Europe at the time of WWII, my brain went "Jewish. War. Concentration camps." I just knew that there would be a lot more to discover about this fascinating woman.

I went online, bought the 4 DVD box set and binge-watched it within days as soon as I had it delivered. I'll watch just one more episode… just one more… I had to force myself to actually go to bed and get some sleep.

I love everything about APTCH, the stories, the characters, the scenery, the outfits, … but I have to say that Sarah's character, and Marta's sublime acting, were what just kept me going. Her and Elizabeth's changing relationship was just fabulous to watch.

I know that every fan has a story arch which moves them, because it reminds them of a loved one or a time in their life. I had one of those too, which was Sarah & Rene's storyline. Way before I ever heard of APTCH, I had heard a story from my Nan about her Dad. She told us that my great-grandfather fought in the First World War, he was part of the Belgian cyclist brigade, delivering messages between different parts of the frontline. He got caught in shell-fire and was badly wounded, especially to the head. He was taken to the military hospital in Nieuwpoort where – as family legend goes – he was nursed by Queen Elisabeth of Belgium. They operated on him and removed as much of the shrapnel from his head as they possibly could, but some was left in. After the war, he met my great-grandmother and they had 3 girls, one of which was my Nan. My Nan said that he was a lovely man but that he could have violent outbursts and terrible mood swings at times. During those episodes, he would shout at my Great Grandmother, shouting that he could feel the shrapnel moving and he'd hit himself. When I saw that portrayed by René, I was just flabbergasted. But the similarities didn't end there. When my Great Grandmother was pregnant with their fourth daughter, his health deteriorated and the headaches & violent outbursts became more frequent. He was hospitalized at the military hospital in Leuven. One day, my Great Grandmother, still very much pregnant, visited him and he attacked her. He pushed her against the door and started strangling her. They needed 4 nurses and doctors to pry him off her and he was then shackled to the bed. Sadly enough, a few days later, he had a brain infection (meningitis) and he passed away. The scene where René attacks Sarah, thinking she's George, was just too eerie to watch because of the similarities. But maybe that's why I have a soft spot for René's character, because it reminds me of my Great Grandfather's story.

But APTCH is so much more than just a very good drama series. I found it so compelling, that I just had to find out if there were any other fans out there, as no one I knew had ever heard of this series – and many still haven't… Just so that I could talk about it! I was desperate! The last time I was so enthralled by a series, was back in the Nineties with the X-Files. And I was young then, so that seemed more acceptable to be a huge fan of a TV series. But surely not a grown 40-odd something? When I found a APTCH fan club on Facebook, I was delighted to find like-minded people who, just like me, had just been enthralled by this series and loved it as much, or more, than I did. It was amazing to hear about the stories of how it was saved by fans, the stories about the cast, the discussions about the characters & story lines, … The hardest part was to avoid the spoilers, as Season 5 was due to start soon on the BBC and the Australians had already obviously seen that series. But equally, the shared anticipation of Season 6, sharing stories, being sad that it was all coming to an end… It was all just wonderful.

And I still love the community page, and the series, as much as I did back in 2018. I have made some great friends, discovered a lot of new Aussie series, but the biggest gift APTCH has given me, is the discovery of Marta Dusseldorp. I think she's one of the most underrated actresses out there. And through the Marta fan page on Facebook, I have made even more friends.

Once this pandemic is over, and I've saved enough money, I am visiting Australia, do an APTCH pilgrimage, and I know that, wherever I'll go in Australia, I'll have friends in every corner of that beautiful country. All thanks to APTCH.

JANE SULLIVAN

I was the first member of the Intl page to make the trip to Oz, so the page admin named me "ambassador." I posted as much as I could, and the members seemed to enjoy living vicariously.

Met up with people at Macca's (McDonald's) before the screening- my old pals Brenda, Margaret and Joel, plus a lot of new friends, who I knew by name, but now for real. Decor was different, fries the same, nuggets a bit better.

The screening was at a movie theatre not unlike the Fox, but smaller, and with several other screens. Still, big enough that there were lots of empty seats. The gang got me a seat front row, center, lots of legroom. I was one of several who got interviewed by Foxtel. Don't know what they will use the footage for, but Brenda recorded it, too, and posted it on the fan page. I got lots of compliments, so I feel good about my ambassador-ing.

The stars came out on stage, sat and autographed a LOT of pictures. The line was so long and there was a big step up to the stage, so I I didn't get to talk to any of them then, just waved at Sara and Jenni, but will at bbq. Bevan Lee, the show's creator was there and gave a little speech, then each star got to talk a bit. The stars acknowledged other crew members - the director, costumer, etc. and then Sara Wiseman , who plays Carolyn Bligh, gave me a shoutout and I had to stand up and wave. Bevan sent Susan Cohen an email and told her he was really impressed that there was a lady all the way from Atlanta, GA. He wants to meet me at the bbq. (!) Pretty unbelievable- the creator of the show wants to meet me!

Now it borders on absurd. Getting to the bbq was going to be a major hassle because they are working on the train tracks. So I got up enough nerve to ask Vanessa, the PR lady, if there was anybody in Sydney that I could catch a ride with. Friday morning I wake up to an email saying that Foxtel (the network produces the show) is sending a car and driver. A huge relief for me, a minor detail for them, I'm sure. WAIT- IT GETS BETTER!

I will not be the only passenger. She sent me the arrangements later in the afternoon, and also in the car will be Graham Burrells, head of Showcase, the channel that the show airs on. I am riding with a big-time exec! I laugh every time I think about it.

There's a little bit of laughter in Marta's play, but mostly her performance is gut-wrenching and intense. I waited after the show to speak to her. No other celebs around this time. I told her I just wanted to check on her since she had seemed so tired Wednesday. She has two shows today and then has to spend her day off schmoozing at the bbq- not much of a day off.

I know she'd rather be playing with her children. Hopefully the fans will show her enough love that it will energize her, not drain her. I will do my best.

Today I will go out and enjoy some Sydney sunshine. Hope you all are having your own wonderful adventure

BBQ- Part 2

People were allowed in at 10:30, and we had morning tea. People mingled outside, but I waited inside. Then we all found a table- I got one near the front, next to the stars' table. Graham gave us the plan for the day - touring Camelot in groups while others could play croquet on the lawn and get autographs from the stars. Then I read selected bits from my poem. Fortunately the stars were still outside. They could hear me, but I didn't have the pressure of performing right in front of them. Then they were introduced one by one and took the stage - not sure who got the biggest applause, Jenni (the villain we love to hate)or Bevan (the show's creator.) They all had chance to say a little something, then Tim Draxl entertained us with four songs.

Great voice, great entertainer.

Yesterday was maybe the most amazing day I have ever had.

Foxtel treated me royally - thank you, Vanessa Hollins, for arranging everything. She arranged for a car and driver to get me to Ash Park. But I was not the only passenger- I got to ride with Graham Burrells, Foxtel exec - head of Foxtel's Premium Entertainment division, which Showcase is part of. He was the emcee at the bbq - a lovely man, so easy to talk to. He and his partner David and Troy, our driver took excellent care of me the whole day. (Troy had recently driven Hugh Jackman, and then Billy Crystal, around. At least he didn't have to help them get around like he did me.)

Graham immediately wanted to know how I found out about APTCH. I told him about the FB fan page. we talked about other shows, like Wentworth, and I read him the beginning of the poem I wrote for the essay contest. He liked it so much that he asked me to read it at the bbq. We got to Ash Park a little early, so we had time to get pictures before everybody else arrived. We were standing out front when two of the stars arrived, Noni Hazlehurst (major star, in the Hall of Fame)and Brett Climo. arrived, so when they got out of the car, I grinned at Noni and said, "Welcome to Ash Park!" She and Brett were absolutely delightful. You'll notice in the photo that I didn't need my cane when I had the two of them!

We got back for lunch. I had left my purse under the table thinking that we were going back to our same seats, but no, our seats weren't saved. There was no guarantee of who would sit where for lunch. I got my purse, and people were in the food line, but I saw Bevan eating and no one else was at his table yet, so I sat down to talk to him. Somebody brought me food and the next thing I knew; I was having lunch with our favorite stars. We all chatted together very easily and they were quite welcoming. I never had a chance to feel like an interloper. Of all the amazing experiences I have had on this trip, all the bonuses I could never have imagined when I bought my plane ticket, this has to be the top. I was living the dream!!! It may never happen for anybody else like it happened for me. Not sure how I got to be lucky one, but I am very, very appreciative. You people living this vicariously, imagine the greatest moment you have ever had, then multiply that pleasure, and you might get an inkling of what I was feeling. Okay, I didn't see Lucky, (the dog)or get selfies with the stars (love your pics, Kirrily) but I got SO much more. Bevan on one side, Noni on the other. On the way home we were joined by Noni and <u>Vanessa Hollins</u>. I'm kinda glad we got stuck in traffic. Reminded me of home- and I got to spend more time chatting with these wonderful people.

On the way home, Vanessa and Noni joined us, so I got some more nice visiting time. I just can't believe all this really happened.

I went to the Jewish Museum. The exhibit that I wanted to see was closed but I did see a very moving collection of letters and postcards. On the way home, I had the cabdriver take the scenic route so we could go by one of the locations I most wanted to see.

…Thursday was another great day of adventure with Brenda. I took the train out to Leppington. She drove me around to a lot of the locations. It was so much fun to sit at the train station where so many scenes had been filmed, including one from this season's opener, where Brenda is an extra, to drive down the road where Sarah rides her bike, etc. The memories of so many wonderful scenes kept flooding through me.

Then, as a special bonus, one that I did not anticipate, she drove me to see some of the Blue Mountains, which are not far from her house. Fabulous scenery, but very, very windy!

And now I'm off for another big day of fun. Brenda has arranged a lunch gathering, and there will be about 20 people, some coming from so far away that they had to catch a train at 7:30. Then we have special access to a parade on Chinatown (Margaret has connections.)

Trains Station and Blue Mountains

The first time I saw Marta's play, Jenni Baird was there, too. Next to Jenni is Lisa Meagher, the costume designer for APTCH. The young girl is Chloe Bayliss, who was in the play, and whom I have seen in other tv shows since. They were all going out afterwards and were kind enough to walk with me to get me a cab. I had Jenni on one arm and Marta on the other!!!

PART THREE: THE FACEBOOK COMMUNITY

Despite the fact that the show ended in 2018, the Facebook group is still growing and very active. What do we talk about? How do we keep it interesting? There are many ways, including a weekly episode discussion, in depth character discussions, speculation posts, polls, and dissection of the smallest things. Fans have been inspired to create poetry or artwork .COVID -19 brought a whole new group of fans to the Community, and each new person brings a possibility of new questions or insights.

The following pages contain just a sampling of the kinds of discussions that we've had.

THE WEEKLY EPISODE POST

Ronni Krasnow

· January 19 · 😬

WEEKLY EPISODE DISCUSSION
Season 3, episode 9: "The Mourner's Kadish"

Sarah mourns Rene

Regina convinces George not to attend Rene's funeral

Doris asks the rabbi about a minyan

Regina informs Sarah that she and George are married

James and Olivia have new sleeping arrangements

Douglas visits Ash Park

Gino finds Anna's novel

Regina learns the baby is George's

George is still using morphine to dull his pain

Gino sells Stardust without asking Anna

Gino and Anna argue over her novel and Anna gets pushed and bangs her head

Regina drugs George's drink and consummates the marriage

This episode gets to me more each time I watch it. So much sadness, and also so much compassion. Marta is amazing in this episode, with that combination of restrained grief, strength, and just utter exhaustion so clearly written on her face. When she says "everything is just too damn late", it breaks my heart. And, of all the evil things Regina has done, I think perhaps revealing the marriage at the moment she did is perhaps the cruelest of all.   The range of wordless emotion on Marta's face when she hears that news is just amazing. When Sarah screams "LIAR", it's the most unleashed she

Jenny Montgomery
Sarah to Regina. "Take this woman from this house".

Like · Reply · 6w 2

Eileen Everitt
Sarah to George, " go home George, go home to your wife". Soooo heartbreaking.

Like · Reply · 6w

Susan Lobel
I think more then in any other episode, Doris and Roy showed the kind of friendship they were both capable of, just sublime!

Like · Reply · 6w

Birthe Ømark
There is so much heartbreak in this episode - but also such amazing acting. All actors are so brilliant and so are all episodes. However, Marta is sublime and at her best portraying Sarah and her grief very convincingly. Sara also has a great performan... **See More**

Like · Reply · 6w · Edited

Laurie Wright
The expression on Sarah's face when she was saying the prayer and heard the car doors! Her pause and then saying(Thank You For Coming All This Way) Such gratitude! This to me helped with the reconciliation and closure she needed! Marta was outstanding ... **See More**

Like · Reply · 6w

THE CHARACTER DISCUSSION POST

CHARACTER STUDY: This week we're talking about the one and only Elizabeth Bligh. As always, you can answer any or all of these prompts as well as share any other thoughts you have:

BEST QUALITY: The ability to (finally) own up to her mistakes and make a genuine change. I think the character development of Elizabeth is the best I have ever seen, bar none.

LEAST ATTRACTIVE QUALITY: Meddling in the lives of her children and grandchildren.

FAVORITE COSTUME: The suit she wore at the wedding toast for her and Douglas.

FAVORITE SCENE (acting wise) When she tries to stop herself from crying about Douglas's illness.

FAVORITE SCENE (story wise) : On the balcony with Sarah at the end of season 4.

BEST LINE: She has so many! "Sometimes fear needs fearing more than the thing we fear", followed by "I have misjudged you" (to Sarah, FINALLY)

AFTER THE SHOW ENDS, THIS CHARACTER: Made the absolute most of the three years she had left, devoting time to the women's home, and also visiting George, Sarah, and David in Israel, and James in France

👍 Like   💬 Comment

Susan Lobel
Best quality, Her ability to change through the seasons of the episode. Least attractive quality: Her stubbornness, but then she learned to channel that a lot. Best costume: The dress Deliah helped her pick out with her new hair do,,though I LOVED her... **See More**

Like · Reply · 41w   👍 1

Sharon Mancini
Best Quality: Ability to change from Elizabeth to Lizzie. Least Attractive Quality: Holding her children/grandchildren to such high standards and trying to run their lives. Favorite Costume: Outfit she wore to Jack & Caro's wedding. Favorite Acting Sce...
See More

Like · Reply · 41w · Edited   👍 1

Lynda Cumiskay
Fabulous actress.Xx
👍 1

Like · Reply · 41w

Suzanne Walters
I love everything about her. To me she's the most rounded fleshed out character. It's a study in growth of the human spirit. She's a beacon of light. She shows we are all capable of redemption and change for the better. All the things that she does whi... **See More**

Like · Reply · 41w   👍 1

Brandy Blackshear

FROM MARILYN MATTHEWS
ELIZABETH

Elizabeth Bligh, A woman who embarked on this journey suited in armor, within her fortified walls. An ardent believer, and advocate for "classism"... Her life was dedicated to what she saw as her duty.... protecting her ideals, and her family....She had quite a few epiphanies along the way, and her fortress and armor began to crumble. I love the way she embraced change... The way she admitted she had done wrong to Carolyn and Jack, and how sorry she was. This enabled her to forge a much-needed relationship between the two women, something they both needed. Every child needs to know their mother loves them. Admitting to Sarah, she had wronged her was a huge step for her. Seeking forgiveness, owning her wrong doings, accepting people no matter their socioeconomic status, learning to release the stranglehold she had on her family, for me are her best qualities. .... My favourite scene was when she sat Sarah and gave her the diagnosis from her GP about her health and telling Sarah she loved her. All had been forgiven and forgotten by these two former adversaries. Beautiful moment....Another fovourite scene was after Douglas' death when she was sitting alone engaged in self-analysis. Asking herself had she done the right by being Lizzie, and not Elizabeth Bligh, ...perhaps if she was the latter, he would have been with her...was she right to give up control....And the big question...who was she after all this.... She delivered many lines that I love. But when she was chatting with Delia, and she said " we can see wrong where it is, in ourselves, and in others, and respond for the good".". Matters are too complex to be trivialized to a battle of the sexes". That entire chat with Delia spoke volumes as to how far Elizabeth had come. ..... I hope she got to spend quality time with The family, especially the Grands.... And the women's home helped many young girls , meeting and fulfilling all of her expectations. Her life had indeed become a blessing to those around her. .... I hope she and Prudence had some fun times together, living life without restrictions....

FROM DONNA ROBINSON DIVINE:

The initial shipboard encounter between wealthy landowner, Elizabeth Bligh and Sister Sarah Adams portrays the power of class in what is said and what is left unsaid. In the very first episode, Elizabeth demands that Sarah tell no one about James' suicide attempt. Sarah responds by emphasizing the importance of providing James with ongoing professional care. Sarah never explicitly promises not to disclose what happened. Yet Elizabeth insists that when Sarah informs George of James' aborted suicide, she broke a promise she made on board the ship. By treating Sarah's silence as a form of consent, Elizabeth stiches a set of assumptions into a narrative of class differences. There is not even a note of uncertainty about Sarah's presumed compliance injected into Elizabeth's reaction or in its retelling.

THE "ALWAYS FINDING SOMETHING NEW" POST

Sharon Mancini
☕ · January 15 · 🙂 ⋯

We always say how much we pick up when we rewatch our show. I'm in my 9th time and just learned something new. I'm curious as to how many others picked it up at one time or another. The question: What is Sir Richard's wife's first name?

👍 6   14 Comments

👍 Like   💬 Comment

View 1 more comment

Brandy Blackshear 💬
I don't know.

Like · Reply · 7w

Birthe Ømark 💬
No idea 🙃

Like · Reply · 7w

View 7 more comments

Write a comment...   🙂 📷 GIF 🖼️

THE "QUESTIONS ABOUT MINUTE DETAILS" POST

 APTCH Community - A Place To Call Home

Does anybody know what the sashes are that are hanging in the hallway at ash park?

👍 5   7 Answ

👍 Like   💬 Comment

'iew 5 more comments

 Lynette Newton
The ribbons would probably be for their wool and champion sheep as they ran a sheep property - although Anna rode I didn't get the impression she did it on a competitive basis. The prize ribbons on show would have indicated to Ash Park visitors how hig... **See More**

👍 3

Like · Reply · 4w

THE SPECULATION POSTS

Brandy Blackshear

· August 7, 2020 ·

Speculation Game: Birthday edition.

We don't see any birthday celebrations during the show. But they are fun to think about.

Tell me about a character's best birthday, or worst birthday, or typical birthday... does one character go particularly all out? Does one character hope nobody ever remembers?

Anything goes, discuss:

👍 Like　　　　　💬 Comment

 Brandy Blackshear
Elaine's first birthday?

At Ash Park or at Harry's farm? Other locations?

Like · Reply · 30w

 Brandy Blackshear 💬
I'd like to think of Elizabeth and Douglas celebrating at least one birthday on their travels sitting outside eating fabulous food and enjoying a fabulous life. Elizabeth deserved that at least once.

Like · Reply · 30w　　　　　👍 4

 Sharon Mancini ☕
It is 1980 and Elaine Bligh has just celebrated her 21st birthday. All her birthdays had been special but this one was absolutely the best. Her mother, Anna, and her grandmother, Carolyn, had been planning it for months. They asked her opinion about ce... **See More**

Like · Reply · 30w · Edited　　　　　👍 8

↳ View 3 more replies

 Cindy Harvey Eager
Absolutely beautiful

Like · Reply · 29w

View 13 more comments

THE "I JUST DISCOVERED THE SHOW" POST

APTCH Community - A Place To Call Home

 Eric Scott Cooper
February 16 at 11:25 AM · 🙂   ● ● ●

Hi everyone! I just finished the entire series yesterday on Acorn TV. I live in in the United States in Los Angeles. It's so funny because I had been avoiding this show on streaming for several years. The poster art for the first season or two makes it look overly wholesome and possibly treacly. I kind of thought it was going to be like one of those Hallmark Channel original series. Not that there's anything wrong with them, but most are just not my style. Boy was I wrong - this show was edgy and pushed the envelope in the best possible sense. I'm so happy I finally went for it. What an amazing show, from start to finish! There were a few small bumps along the way, as with any series. But overall, just high quality and interesting story lines throughout. Great performances, fantastic writing, beautiful costumes, set design and art direction. And there was very impressive incorporation of various social and political issues. It shows how much has changed in society and, sadly, how little. I'm thrilled to be here and I'm glad that this forum is still active. I just love love love the show so much and can't stop trying to convince my friends to give it a go! 🍷🤗👍🖤☮️

👍❤️ 79   85 Comments

👍 Like   💬 Comment

View 33 more comments

THE "KEEPING UP WITH ALL THE ACTORS" POST

 Nat Hedington shared a post.
May 4, 2019 ·

Marta has finished filming her scenes for Ellie and Abbie ☺

THE HOW DID YOU FEEL WHEN...POST

 APTCH Community - A Place To Call Home

 Gaylene Parish
 · January 31 · 🌐   •••

Does anyone else wish that Sarah had held her tongue at the election rally - would have prevented Richard's terrible attack on Jack.   It also seems out of character for her.

 2   15 Comments

👍 Like   💬 Comment

View 9 more comments

 Brandy Blackshear
I think Sarah can be a total know it all who gets all up in peoples business when it shouldn't concern her (it is both part of her charm and the bit that bugs me about her) but I don't think she was at fault at all in this instance. Sir Richard was go... **See More**

Like · Reply · 4w   👍 2

 Helen Bell
I am sure Sarah would have said something at some point. The fact that she did, when she did, also opened up to Sir Richard's attack on Regina. Her outcome may have been so different as well. A whole different story line if Regina hadn't taken the step... **See More**

Like · Reply · 4w

THE OMG WE'RE DOING ANOTHER ZOOM CHAT POST

 Fran Simmons

Admin +1 · July 17, 2020 · 😊   •••

Here's some news on the next Zoom chat guest on the SAPTCH group!

"Hi Everyone!

Hot on the heels of our wonderful zoom interviews with Noni Hazlehurst and Bevan Lee, We would like to announce a new guest.

Reserve a spot on your couch, as on Saturday July 25 at 8:30pm we will be having an evening with the Foxy crooner himself, Mr Tim Draxl.

Tim won us over as Dr Henry Fox on APTCH 🦊 but did you know he is also one of Australia's favourite stage and cabaret artists who has been entertaining us during lockdown.

If you missed him here is a sneaky link to The Sydney Opera House Digital Season featuring our Foxy Crooner
https://www.sydneyoperahouse.com/.../tim-draxl-live.html...

So, If you would like to ask Tim a question then here's your chance! Please ask your question, here, on this thread and we will send your questions to Tim.

We have a limit of 100 people on a Zoom chat. The same guidelines for the chat with Bevan and Noni will apply to the chat with Tim. The chat will open at 8pm and we need everyone online by 8:15

If your question is chosen then you'll get to ask it to Tim, but you have to be at the chat. We will confirm your question has been selected on this thread. If you are unable to make the chat please let us know and we will ask your question on your behalf if there is time.

THE HISTORICAL DISCUSSIONS POST

 APTCH Community - A Place To Call Home

 Catherine Nyhan Cheney

Admin · February 14 at 4:50 PM · 😔 ···

Many of you have seen Fran's post with the message from Bevan Lee. In it, he mentioned that a possible discussion topic (see attached photo) regarding the similarities between the current pandemic and the Spanish Flu Pamdemic, which some of the characters would have lived through. So, let's take his cue and discuss.

been a comfort to many during these difficult times. He had this to say to you all:

"My thoughts are with everyone, as Covid sadly continues far beyond what we had imagined when it first appeared. An interesting thought is that Elizabeth Bligh, Roy Briggs and Doris Collins would all have experienced similar dangers and fears during the Spanish Flu outbreak of 1918 to 1920. It's an interesting exercise to imagine how that outbreak might have impacted the lives of those characters, how similar to the now of us and how different due to different times. This might serve as a discussion topic for you all, and a focus of some interesting historical research."

LITERARY REFERENCE POSTS

FROM MARILYN MATTHEWS

Loved when Sarah, was standing on the Verandah awaiting George's arrival with joyful anticipation... He arrives, and looks at her with love, tenderness, and such longing in his eyes, it warmed the cockles of my heart, I can imagine what happened with theirs. This episode always makes me think of English Literature classes, the Romantic Poets.... The moment they busted through the doors and started undressing each other, I thought of these lines in Romeo and Juliette. "Love is a smoke and is made with the fume of sighs" There was a lot of smoke in that room........ I loved when they were just lying there being comforted, and enjoying each other's presence, for me that is very romantic. .When Sarah told George she never imagined the first night he brought her there, she never imagined they would be there together, and he said he knew he wanted her the moment he took her in his arms to dance was so honest, that's one of the things I like about them, their honesty with each other, no BS, they get straight to the point. ....

FROM HAGIT CARMEL

<u>A Poem and Homage</u>
This is the poem that Sarah was reading to Roy on Yom-Kippur, defining it as "Rene's favourite".
The poem is by Federico Garcia Lorca

From here
Tell my friends that I've died.
Tell them that I'm out here in the sky, my eyes wide open.
My face covered up by this endless blue shroud.
That I've gone off, empty, to the stars.

And Here is the homage:
Here
Tell the stars my soul is covered
With a cloak of saneness in the skies.
Tell them my body is dipping in water
With closed and longing p

119

POETRY AND ART

A TRIBUTE TO A PLACE TO CALL HOME

by Jane Sullivan

One evening last spring I saw on TV
An Australian show that appealed to me.
"A Place to Call Home" looked very inviting.
I had no idea it would be so exciting.

At first lured in by the beautiful sets,
The music, the costumes - I had no regrets
About spending so much time engrossed in the tales
Of the family Bligh, in New South Wales.

Each had their challenges in learning to live
In a changing country, and how each could give
Their best to the future yet respects the past.
Changes were coming- some too slow, some too fast.

I love how we see the culture evolve,
But the same issues today we have yet to resolve.
Same-sex relationships, post-war trauma,
Religious intolerance, all make riveting drama.

With plot lines full of secrets and lies
Each episode reveals a well-crafted surprise.
The writing is stellar, the characters compelling.
Each season gets better in its storytelling.

Ash Park at sunset or at sunrise
Is lushly filmed, a treat for the eyes.
A spectacular house, it couldn't be grander.
(Though I'd rather have a beer on Roy's veranda.)

The collection of cars is fun to behold,
But riding those bikes is tricky, I'm told,
Especially in one's Sunday array,
As Sarah was on christening day.

I love the bond between Sarah and Lucky.
When Sarah said, "Get her!" and with plenty of pluck he
Went after Regina, Sarah and I both smiled a big smile -
Regina had to back off at least for a while.

Ah, Regina - where do I start?
She's conniving, ambitious, she thinks she's so smart
To have seduced poor George in a morphine haze.
That's not even the worst of her diabolical ways.

Poisoning Sarah was the most despicable deed.
In a recent poll most people agreed
That Regina has to go. Though we love to hate her,
She needs her comeuppance- sooner, not later.

Elizabeth started out antagonistically,
But true to her upbringing, she acted realistically.
As her actions were thwarted, she softened a lot.
Will she live to find love, or die on the spot?

I want more of Carolyn and her life in the city.
What Sir Richard did to her was really, really sh__ty.
With her charm and her sparkle, she should rule the town
And have all the right contacts to bring Dickie down.

Jack will surely get out of the charges falsely claimed -
It's obvious somebody wanted him to be framed.
Can he and Carolyn imitate real life
And become the perfect couple - truly husband and wife?

As for Anna and Gino, Olivia and James,
I think Bevan is taunting us with clever mind games.
I dare not prognosticate, but I wish each the best.
Does that mean staying together, facing each test?

Roy can be counted on for total support-
I'd like to see his role have greater import.
And what role for George- Ash Park or politics?
It won't be easy escaping Regina's bag of tricks.

I love all the characters, but I have to confess
That Sarah is the one about whom I obsess.
From the very first scene, in each hand a suitcase,
She captivated me with her beauty and grace.

A remarkable talent is Marta D.,
Who portrays Sister Adams exquisitely?
Whatever the role calls for, she's up to the task,
Want to take down Bert Ford? Who better to ask!

With shotgun or horse she's equally proficient,
And as community nurse she is caring and efficient.
I watched with delight her budding romance
With handsome George Bligh, from that first shipboard dance.

They brought to each other a happiness once lost
In Japanese bombings and the German Holocaust.
But alas, their blissfulness was not to be,
Thanks to evil Regina's skullduggery.

Sarah's love for Rene would never waver or bend,
But we all knew his death had to come in the end.
Will she get back with George some time in Season Four,
Or can Bevan draw this out for many seasons more?

The wait is excruciating, I'm on needles and pins,
And I share this anticipation with my new Facebook friends.
We binge-watch whenever, thanks to Acorn and streaming,
Of a trip to Australia is what we're all dreaming.

To the cast and the crew, as filming gets under way,
May this year be the best. Now I bid you "G'Day!"

LENA NORRMAN:

FAN FICTION

PRUDENCE THROWS A PARTY

by Jane Sullivan

Prudence Swanson beamed as the guests began arriving. She loved throwing parties, particularly when the guest list held such illustrious names. Sir Robert and Dame Pattie Menzies were there, but even the Prime Minister had to take a back seat this time. Today was a fundraiser for the planned Sydney Opera House, and Prudence had arranged an appearance by one of the opera world's brightest stars, Joan Sutherland, back in Australia for a brief visit after her smashing success at London's Royal Opera House, where her aria from Handel's Samson had garnered a ten-minute-long standing ovation.

Next to Prudence and smiling even more broadly were Elizabeth and Douglas Goddard. The fundraiser was Douglas' idea. He had enthusiastically embraced Eugene Goossen's vision of a large performing arts venue to be built on Bennelong Point, and continued to promote the idea even after the symphony conductor's hasty departure once his pornography scandal was revealed. Two years had passed, the scandal had receded, and it was time to push forward on this grand project.

A string quartet provided a melodious background to the spirited buzz of conversations all around the grounds. Carolyn Duncan's engaging laugh could be heard in many places as she easily maneuvered from group to group, trailed by her dutiful husband Jack. He was much more at ease with his patients in Inverness than he was in Sydney society.

Jack searched the crowd for any familiar face, someone he could talk to. He perked up when he saw George Bligh. Thank goodness, someone from home. Maybe he could just talk to George and not worry about small talk with strangers. And if Sarah were with him, so much the better. Yes, there she was. Jack headed in their direction. Elizabeth had noticed how Jack visibly relaxed when he saw George and Sarah. She knew he didn't really like these society affairs. For some reason he was always a little afraid he would embarrass himself, and she never wanted him to feel that way.

Elizabeth had felt very differently at the party she and Prudence had thrown for Pattie Menzies when she became a dame. That day Elizabeth fervently had hoped that someone would be embarrassed and shown to be out of her depth. But Sarah Adams had charmed everyone at that party, especially Dame Pattie. Elizabeth had conceded defeat that day, and her grudging respect had turned to genuine, deep affection over the next months. And now, finally, Sarah and

George were married. George had given up politics in order to stay at home, but he had gotten a bit restless, and was looking for something new in which to invest his time and interest. Perhaps the answer was right here at this party.

The architect of the Opera House, Jorn Utzon of Denmark, was not at the fundraiser, but several other important people were, most notably Dick Dusseldorp, who had won the contract to build the podium. George was quite anxious to meet him and hear about his new company, Civil and Civic. Dusseldorp had quite progressive ideas on how to run a company, and George wanted to learn as much as possible. Sarah was also interested in meeting the Dutch immigrant. She knew that he had been a prisoner of war, and felt an immediate kinship with him, although neither talked about their war experiences.

The three were so engrossed in conversation that Jack reluctantly turned away without trying to interrupt. He turned to face the person he despised more than anyone else in the world, Sir Richard Bennett. Sir Richard looked at Jack, and grinned a slow, condescending grin. He knew his presence would make Jack miserable, so he decided to stay as near to Jack as he could for the remainder of the party. Jack was afraid he would lose his temper and embarrass Elizabeth and Prudence. He knew Carolyn wouldn't dare get close to Sir Richard again. Four years had passed since that awful night, and Jack's relationship with Carolyn had grown even deeper as they overcame the trauma together, but Carolyn could not bear even to hear Sir Richard's name, much less be anywhere near him. Suddenly, the grin disappeared from Sir Richard's face, and he began to work his way to the exit. Jack turned around and saw Elizabeth, standing with a devilish look in her eye and a fruit knife in her hand.

Prudence and the other guests were oblivious to that little scene. By all accounts, the party was a great success. A great amount of champagne was drunk, an even greater amount of money was raised, and everyone was enchanted by Joan Sutherland's rendition of "Let the Bright Seraphim."

CATHERINE CHENEY

Exclusive to Vineyards Monthly – April 2017
Poletti Winemakers Discover Family Ties

A new generation is at the helm of Poletti Wineries, more than 50 years after patriarch Gino Poletti planted his first vines in the fertile Napa Valley soil. Thirty-seven-year-old Gina Poletti is the 3rd generation of Poletti Winemakers in charge of the largest producer of Sangiovese (often called California Chianti) in America. She takes over from her father, Angelo, and his twin brother, Amo, who, at age 63, are ready to take life a little easier. Both will remain involved in the Winery in a lesser role.

As the only child of this generation interested in the family business, Gina has been searching for a trusted business partner for several years. When her path crossed with Eve Walker (age 36), their mutual love and knowledge of wine bonded them instantly. Soon they discovered that they both had more than wine running through their veins…they also had Poletti blood.

The journey of discovery came when the winery's founder, Gino, was introduced to Eve shortly before his death last year at the age of 88. He told Gina that he had known a woman named Eve Walker when he was a young man in Australia. This remark led present-day Eve to admit that that she'd been named after her paternal grandmother, but never knew who either of her grandfathers was. Only after Gino's passing did his wife Rose tell Eve that she had indeed met her grandfather – Gino.

Eve, who became an American citizen soon after graduating from the University of Washington's' Viticulture program, was prompted to visit her native Australia to piece together her story. What she discovered was of as much interest to her new business partner as it was to herself.

Gino had never confided in his children that he had had a short-lived marriage to Anna Bligh, prior to meeting Rose – his wife of 60 years. The shame of divorcing Anna, believing she was unable to bear children led to his immigration to California. He learned years later that Anna had given birth to Gino's daughter 8 months after their split. Whatever he may have felt about this discovery was buried beneath the pressures of raising his young family with Rose and an increasingly successful wine business.

"I was really just a child when I came to America to attend University", admitted Eve. "I had a wonderful childhood. Despite the age difference between my parents, Colin and Elizabeth, they were well suited for one another. They had met at University, when mum was a student and Dad a professor. Mum also joined the faculty, as a music teacher, and they were married. I spent a lot of time in Sydney with my grandmother, Anna Duncan, who was a pioneer in the field of television, earning a lifetime achievement award for script writing. Anna took the surname of her birth father in order to distance herself and her unconventional (at the time) career from her father George's burgeoning political career, and so I never knew of her first, and only, marriage."

Prior to Eve's arrival in Australia, learning of Rose's revelation prompted Elizabeth Walker to do something she'd never done before – look into the story of her parentage. "There were times when I did wonder about my father", Elizabeth said. My dark hair and olive skin were so different than my mother's. But my childhood was full of father figures, especially my uncle James and his long-time companion, Henry. I spent holidays at the Bligh family home with my cousin George, and my uncle David, who is just a year older than I am. I had a large, loving family, but now, in my 60's, I had new questions. My mother lives at Ash Park with a carer, suffering from advanced Alzheimer's, and it was David who finally provided me with the truth. David's mother, Sarah, had confided in him, but asked him never to reveal who the father of Anna's child was unless and until it appeared important to do so. Apparently, he considered Eve's sudden arrival from America reason enough to tell me what he knew. I admit that I was surprised, but I was more surprised that Eve and Gina had found each other, in another part of the world, without having any clue that they are related.

Gina has now been reunited with her Aussie relatives via Skype and the news has caused a buzz of excitement through the Poletti Winery. Though Anna Bligh Poletti Duncan now lives in the fog of dementia, her daughter and granddaughter sat and shared the story with her recently. They were both astounded to see a rare smile cross her face as she uttered "Poletti wines – for that special occasion".

CONCLUSION
DONNA ROBINSON DIVINE

Today, three years after APTCH ended its run, one of the administrators of the Facebook Community Page welcomed eight new members. One can attribute the continued interest in the program to the lockdowns imposed across the globe with people desperately searching for binge-worthy series to watch. But while Covid-19 may have given the program new viewers, it surely could not have generated what is evident in the pages of this collection: the overwhelming need of fans-new and old-to talk about the plot, the characters, their strengths and weaknesses, their joys as they find love and respect and their despair when they encounter rejection and condemnation.

By all accounts, A Place To Call Home allowed iconic characters to enter public consciousness and become worthy of serious consideration. The characters reflected and illuminated the many different experiences during an era when social conventions were challenged and shaken. Facebook posts illustrate how viewers absorbed and assessed the implications of what they saw and heard. The relationships depicted in the series invited viewers to eavesdrop on the kind of conversations that still echo in our own day. The adjectives describing the series' characters embraced by fans in their Facebook posts showed what we all had in common as well as what aversions we still shared. Fans were skilled in understanding the class signifiers of clothes but also of language. As the comments in this collection show, the actors, many well-known for their earlier television hits or some less familiar but seasoned in live theater, were so fully absorbed in their roles as to appear not to be acting but rather to be living at a time and in a place that had once generated only sentimental attachment rather than the kind of critical engagement on offer on television from this series.

The brilliant acting left almost nothing to the imagination. The dialogue, the facial expressions, and the physical contact, placed the audience inside the vivid scenes of past and present. Whether it was sexual abuse, rape, death, fans were made to see and feel the pain and to understand the impact. These extraordinary actors could convey despair with a single look, elevating the unexceptional into moving poignancy. The interactions at times across classes or on other occasions within the family showed how trauma loops through generations stalking those who thought them-selves, by age and circumstance, beyond its reach.

The pivotal character is a survivor of the absolute worst humanity offered and ends up able to show how the world was created for good and that good could still be discerned even amidst what appeared to be more turmoil and violence than human beings could be expected to bear. Despite all obstacles, the struggle for dignity and happiness continues--as it should. When Elizabeth and Douglas return to Ash Park after their marriage, the celebration concludes with the Hebrew words—le Chayim—conventionally translated as "to life". But for the fans who found this story so compelling, the phrase should be deconstructed into its original meaning: for the sake of life, giving all of its fans an abiding sense that despite all difficulties, it is worthwhile to find the spiritual energy from within and without to go one, to assume better days will come not so much by chance but rather because of what we do and who we are.

How to summarize this powerful experience that was as unexpected as it was significant? For all the contributors to these pages, A Place To Call Home was more than a mere TV show. Some needed it to cope with their own difficult times; others for the energy to travel to Australia. Some found inspiration in the series for their art; others, found it the muse for writing poetry. Many who helped save the show were transformed by their activities and by their personal encounters with one another. All gained a deeper understanding of social issues and of cultures unknown to them. Some learned of a history that unfolded before they were born. Most importantly, all of us gained friendships that sustain us and that we want, even plan to transform from virtual to real when we can travel.

For all of this, we thank the administrators of the APTCH Community Facebook site for bringing us together. We are grateful for the extraordinary cast and crew whose talents made an ingenious story powerful and whose interactions with fans have been gracious and generous. And, of course, we wish to express our admiration for Bevan Lee whose story has resonated so deeply and has left all of us in awe of his talent and wishing he had given us more.